THE TIMESAVER COOKBOOK

Recipes compiled by Miriam B. Loo

Photographer—Ron Oatney
Food Stylist—Marjorie Read

Born and raised in Topeka, Kansas, MIRIAM BAKER LOO is an accomplished businesswoman and creative homemaker who has been an enthusiastic cook since her youth. After her graduation from Washburn University of Topeka, from which she recently received the Outstanding Achievement Award, she married Orin Loo, an artist and lithographer. The Loo family later moved to Colorado Springs, Colorado, where in 1950, with the help of her husband, Miriam founded Current, Inc.®

Current is a national mail order firm which has grown from a basement business in the Loo home, when the product line included Post-A-Note® cards and recipe cards designed by Mr. Loo, to a thriving enterprise serving millions of customers.

Miriam Loo introduced recipes into the Current line by including them on note cards and calendars, and now the company publishes several cookbooks each year. In 1979, she established the Current Test Kitchen, which today includes four kitchens and a staff of six home economists who carefully test each Current recipe. She attends gourmet cooking classes and makes public appearances on behalf of Current all over the country, yet she still enjoys cooking and entertaining for her friends and family, including three grown sons and five grandchildren.

Long involved in volunteer activities, Miriam Loo has received national recognition for her accomplishments in community work, church leadership and business.

Pictured on the cover is Chicken Milanese. (See page 62.)

Dear Friends,

In the early days of my marriage and career, I considered myself a very busy person. Now that my everyday household consists of only Orin and me, and my schedule is entirely different, I find that I have as little time as ever! That seems to be the nature of things today: Never enough hours in the day to do the things we have to . . . and want to . . . no matter what stage of life we're in.

In this book I've tried to keep all kinds of cooks in mind. Those who are able to budget their preparation time over several days, those who are always hurried in the kitchen, and those who love to entertain but are constantly on the go.

Don't skip a chapter. There are all kinds of ways to manage your cooking time better, and you'll find many that suit your style. Three of the chapters have menus and work plans to save you the time of sorting through recipes for the perfect combination. The appliance chapter utilizes equipment you may already have, or may want to buy. Get into the habit of using these wonderful devices as often as possible. If you don't have a microwave oven, share these recipes with a friend who does. You both will be pleasantly surprised.

Being a good cook is a challenge, especially when time isn't on your side. My recipes use some convenience products to hurry things along, but only if the results taste homemade. I hope you will find my suggestions and recipes useful and satisfying.

Sincerely,

Miriam B. Loo

TABLE OF CONTENTS

⚱ Indicates preparation required just before serving.

MAKE-AHEAD
MAIN DISHES

Pictured on the preceding page are: Chinese Hens with Orange Rice and Cloverleaf Dinner Rolls.

CHINESE HENS WITH ORANGE RICE

"Cornish hens are always a treat, but in this recipe they are particularly moist and flavorful."

1 cup orange juice ....
2/3 cup dry white wine
1/3 cup soy sauce
1 tablespoon minced gingerroot
1 tablespoon brown sugar

In a shallow glass dish, mix orange juice, wine, soy sauce, gingerroot and brown sugar.

3 Cornish game hens (1 to 1¼ lb. each), halved

Place hen halves in marinade, pressing down firmly to completely cover. Cover and refrigerate for 12 to 24 hours.

1½ cups uncooked regular rice
1½ cups orange juice
½ teaspoon salt

⌂ About 1¼ hours before serving, preheat oven to 450°. Grease a 13 × 9 × 2-inch baking pan. Mix rice, orange juice and salt in baking pan. Place hens, cut-side down, in rice mixture; reserve marinade. Cover and bake for 45 minutes. Uncover and bake 10 to 15 minutes longer or until rice has absorbed all liquid and hens are well browned.

1/3 cup sliced almonds
2 tablespoons butter or margarine
3 green onions, thinly sliced

While hens are baking, in a small skillet over medium heat, sauté almonds in butter or margarine for 2 to 3 minutes or until almonds are golden. Add green onions and sauté for 2 to 3 minutes or until onions are limp but still green; set aside.

continued on next page . . .

Chinese Hens with Orange Rice continued . . .

1 tablespoon . . . . cornstarch	In a medium saucepan, mix reserved marinade and cornstarch until smooth. Stirring over medium heat, bring to a boil and boil for 1 to 2 minutes or until thickened.
1 can (11 oz.) . . . . mandarin orange segments, drained	Transfer hens to a platter. Stir nut mixture and ¾ cup of the orange segments into the rice mixture. Mound rice on platter or in a separate serving bowl.
Parsley sprigs	Spoon some sauce over hens. Garnish platter with remaining orange segments and parsley. Serve remaining sauce separately.

Makes 6 servings

OVERNIGHT BRUNCH EGGS

"My newest entrée for a weekend get-together. See the menu on page 42 for serving ideas."

1 pound Monterey . . . . Jack cheese, shredded (4 cups) 2 tablespoons all-purpose flour	In a medium bowl, toss together cheese and flour. Sprinkle in the bottom of an ungreased 4-quart oblong baking dish.*
12 ounces hot pork . . . . sausage 3 cans (4 oz. each) whole green chilies ½ pound Cheddar cheese, shredded (2 cups)	In a medium skillet over medium-high heat, brown sausage; drain and crumble; set aside. Cut chilies open to lie flat and remove seeds. Layer on top of Monterey Jack cheese. Sprinkle Cheddar cheese over green chilies. Top with sausage.
12 eggs . . . . 1 cup milk	In a medium bowl, beat eggs and milk until well blended. Pour egg mixture over sausage. Cover and refrigerate up to 24 hours.

Uncover and bake in a preheated 350° oven for 40 to 45 minutes or until mixture is puffed and egg custard is set when dish is shaken. Serve immediately.

*Two 2-quart oblong baking dishes may be used. Bake for 30 to 40 minutes.

Makes 12 (3½ × 3-inch) servings

7

TROPICAL CHICKEN SALAD

¾ cup mayonnaise .... In a small bowl, mix mayonnaise, mustard, ginger,
2 teaspoons prepared   sugar, lemon juice and salt until smooth; set aside.
  mustard
2 teaspoons ground
  ginger
2 teaspoons sugar
1 teaspoon lemon juice
¼ teaspoon salt

2 cups diced .... In a medium bowl, mix chicken, oranges, pineapple
  cooked chicken   and celery. Add dressing and stir until evenly coated.
1 can (11 oz.) mandarin Cover and refrigerate for 1 to 24 hours.
  orange segments,
  drained
1 can (8 oz.) pineapple
  tidbits in juice,
  drained
1 cup thinly sliced
  celery

1 cup chow mein ..... Just before serving, stir in noodles. Spoon into let-
  noodles   tuce cups on individual plates if desired.
4 lettuce cups
  (optional)

Makes 4 (1-cup) servings

TURKEY MORNAY

¼ pound Canadian .... Lightly grease a 2½-quart casserole. In a large skillet
  bacon, cut in 1 ×   over medium heat, brown bacon in butter or marga-
  ¼ × ¼-inch strips   rine. Drain bacon on paper towels; set aside.
2 tablespoons butter or
  margarine

¼ pound mush- .... Add mushrooms and onion to skillet; sauté for 2 to
  rooms, sliced   3 minutes or until limp.
1 small onion, chopped

¼ cup all-purpose ..... Stir in flour, thyme and pepper. Cook and stir for 1
  flour   to 2 minutes. Add broth and milk. Stirring, bring to a
½ teaspoon dried   boil and boil until thickened.
  thyme leaves,
  crushed
¼ teaspoon pepper
2 cups chicken broth
1 cup milk

continued on next page . . .

⅓ cup grated . . . . Stir in cheese and sherry;
   Parmesan cheese   simmer for 5 to 6 minutes,
3 tablespoons dry   stirring occasionally
   sherry   (sauce will be thin).

2 cups twist . . . . In a large bowl, place
   macaroni, cooked   bacon, sauce, macaroni,
   and drained   asparagus, turkey or
1 package (8 or 9 oz.)   chicken and 1½ cups of
   frozen asparagus   the mozzarella cheese;
   pieces, thawed and   toss lightly until evenly
   drained   combined. Spoon mix-
1 cup diced cooked   ture into casserole;
   turkey or chicken   sprinkle with remaining
8 ounces mozzarella   cheese. Cover and
   cheese, shredded   refrigerate up to 24 hours
   (2 cups)   (flavor improves with
   standing).

🔔 Bake covered in a preheated 350° oven for 50 to
60 minutes or until bubbly and heated through.

Makes 6 (1-cup) servings

NACHO CHICKEN

8 chicken breast . . . . . . Place one chicken breast half between two pieces of
   halves, skinned   waxed paper. Flatten to ¼-inch thickness with a
   and boned   wooden mallet or a rolling pin. Peel off waxed paper.
   Salt   Sprinkle lightly with salt.

4 whole canned . . . . . . Cut each green chili in half lengthwise. Cut cheese
   green chilies   into eight 1½ × ½ × ½-inch sticks. Wrap one half
2 ounces Monterey   chili around one cheese stick. Place on flattened
   Jack cheese in 1   chicken half and roll up, tucking sides in as you roll
   piece   so no chili or cheese is visible. Secure with wooden
   picks.

⅓ cup butter or . . . . Dip chicken roll in butter or margarine. Roll in crushed
   margarine, melted   chips until well coated. Place seam-side up in an
1 cup finely crushed   ungreased 2-quart oblong baking dish. Repeat with
   nacho tortilla chips   remaining green chilies, cheese sticks and chicken.
   Cover and refrigerate for 2 to 24 hours.

🔔 Uncover and bake in a preheated 400° oven for
20 to 25 minutes or until chicken is no longer pink.
Remove wooden picks before serving.

Makes 8 servings

GLAZED MEAT LOAF

2 cups soft bread crumbs 1 cup milk 1 egg, lightly beaten 2 tablespoons catsup 2 tablespoons prepared mustard 1 teaspoon salt ⅛ teaspoon pepper	In a large bowl, mix bread crumbs, milk, egg, catsup, mustard, salt and pepper. Let stand for 5 minutes.
1½ pounds lean ground beef 12 ounces hot bulk pork sausage 2 tablespoons *each* minced onion and minced parsley	Add ground beef, sausage, onion and parsley; mix well. Divide mixture into four equal portions. Pack one meat mixture portion into each of two ungreased 7½ × 3¾ × 2½-inch foil loaf pans.
8 ounces sharp Cheddar cheese, cut in ¼-inch thick slices	Place half of the cheese in each pan, making sure cheese does not touch sides of pan (or it will ooze out during baking). Cover each with a second portion of meat mixture, packing over cheese. Cover and refrigerate up to 24 hours or freeze up to 1 month.
½ cup catsup ¼ cup sugar ¾ cup chili sauce	About 1¾ hours (2¾ hours if frozen) before serving, preheat oven to 350°. In a small saucepan over medium heat,* bring catsup and sugar to a boil, stirring. Remove from heat. Stir in chili sauce. Brush each

loaf with about ¼ cup of the glaze. Bake uncovered for 1 hour (2 hours if frozen). Turn oven off and let loaves stand 30 minutes longer. Remove from oven and drain off liquid. Serve loaves with remaining warmed glaze.

*If baking one loaf at a time, make only half the glaze mixture.

Makes 2 loaves

Make-Ahead Main Dishes

SPICY BEEF BAKE

"Make two of these for a buffet dinner. Corn bread is a must."

1½ pounds ground beef chuck
1 cup chopped onion
1 large clove garlic, minced

In a large skillet over medium-high heat, sauté beef, onion and garlic just until meat is no longer pink; drain off fat.

1 can (16 oz.) tomato wedges
1 tart apple, peeled, cored and diced
¼ cup raisins
2 tablespoons all-purpose flour
1 teaspoon salt
¼ teaspoon pepper
⅛ teaspoon ground cinnamon
⅛ teaspoon ground cloves

Stir in tomatoes, apple, raisins, flour, salt, pepper, cinnamon and cloves. Spoon into a 1½-quart oblong baking dish. Cover and refrigerate up to 24 hours.

Bake covered in a preheated 400° oven for 25 to 30 minutes or until bubbly.

4 ounces mozzarella cheese, shredded (1 cup)
Pimiento strips

Uncover beef mixture, sprinkle with cheese. Arrange pimiento over cheese. Bake uncovered for 5 minutes or until cheese melts.

Makes 6 servings

ENERGY-SAVING ROAST

"Slice paper thin for excellent sandwiches the next day."

1 boneless beef round tip roast (4 to 5 lb.)

Preheat oven to 375°. Place roast, fat-side up, on a rack in a shallow roasting pan. Do not add water. Do not cover. Roast for 1 hour. Turn oven off, *do not open oven door.* Let stand for up to 4 hours.

Turn oven back on to 375°. Roast for 40 minutes. Remove to serving dish and let stand for 10 to 15 minutes before carving.

Makes 16 to 20 servings

11

RUNZAS

"I discovered this new way to use ground beef on a trip through Nebraska."

1 medium onion, ... In a large skillet over medium heat, sauté onion and
chopped   garlic in oil for 3 to 4 minutes or until limp. Add meat.
2 medium cloves   Cook and stir just until meat is no longer pink; drain
garlic, minced   off liquid.
1 tablespoon vegetable
oil
1 pound lean ground
beef

8 ounces Monterey ... Stir in cheese, sauerkraut, Worcestershire sauce, salt
Jack or sharp   and red pepper; set aside.
Cheddar cheese,
shredded (2 cups)
1 can (8 oz.) sauer-
kraut, rinsed and
drained
1 tablespoon Worces-
tershire sauce
1 teaspoon salt
¼ teaspoon ground red
pepper

Quick Buttery ...... Divide dough into two equal portions. On a lightly
Yeast Dough (see   floured surface, roll one portion into an 18 × 12-inch
page 84)   rectangle. Cut in half lengthwise, then crosswise into
thirds to make six 6-inch squares. Repeat with remaining portion.

Spoon about ⅓ cup of the meat filling onto the center
of each square. Bring corners up over filling to meet
in the middle. Pinch edges together to seal. Place
packets on an ungreased baking sheet; freeze. When
frozen, store in a sealed container or plastic bag up
to 3 months.

🔔 Bake on an ungreased baking sheet in a
preheated 400° oven for 20 to 25 minutes or until
golden brown.

Catsup .... Serve hot with catsup if desired.

Makes 12

NOTES:

TAMALE CORN BREAD PIE

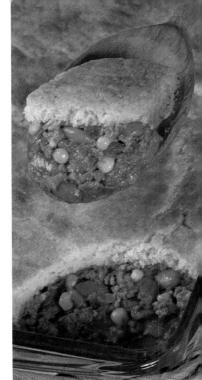

2 medium onions, ... chopped 1 tablespoon vegetable oil	In a large skillet over medium-high heat, sauté onions in oil until limp.
2 pounds lean .... ground beef	Add beef and cook just until brown. Drain off liquid. Place meat mixture in a large bowl.
2 cans (16 oz. .... each) chili beans in chili gravy 1 can (17 oz.) whole kernel corn, drained 1 can (16 oz.) stewed tomatoes 2 cans (4 oz. each) chopped green chilies 2 to 3 teaspoons chili powder ½ teaspoon salt	Add beans in gravy, corn, tomatoes, green chilies, chili powder and salt. Mix well. Divide mixture evenly between two 2-quart oblong baking dishes. Cover and refrigerate up to 24 hours or freeze up to 3 months.
1 box (15 oz.) corn.... bread mix	About 1 hour before serving, uncover and bake in a preheated 400° oven for 20 minutes (45 minutes if frozen) or until mixture is bubbly. Meanwhile prepare corn bread mix according to package directions.* Spread half the batter evenly on top of each baking dish. Return to oven for 10 minutes; reduce heat to 350° and bake 20 to 25 minutes longer or until corn bread is golden brown.

*If baking only one pie, prepare corn bread using half of the mix and half of the other ingredients called for. Reserve the remaining dry corn bread mix until baking the other pie.

Makes 2 pies (six 1-cup servings each)

USING FREEZER PAPER

Freezer paper is specifically designed for protecting your freezer food, but it has other uses . . . waxed-side in, shape paper into a cone for a quick funnel or for a makeshift pastry bag . . . waxed-side out, use freezer paper to cover children's books . . . waxed-side up, use freezer paper as a very sturdy shelf liner, allowing pans and dishes to slide out easily.

PORK SATÉ

½ cup water	In a shallow glass dish, mix water, soy sauce, peanut butter, oil, lemon juice, sugar, garlic, coriander and pepper flakes. Place pork cubes in marinade. Cover and let stand at room temperature for 3 to 4 hours or in refrigerator overnight.
¼ cup soy sauce	
¼ cup chunky peanut butter	
2 tablespoons vegetable oil	
2 tablespoons lemon juice	
1 tablespoon sugar	
2 medium cloves garlic, minced	
1 teaspoon ground coriander	
¼ to ½ teaspoon red pepper flakes	
1 pound pork tenderloin, cut in 1-inch cubes	
8 bamboo skewers . . . . (10 inches long)	Soak skewers in water while meat is marinating. (Skewers will burn less during broiling if water soaked.)
Pineapple chunks . . . Cherry tomatoes	Alternately thread pineapple and tomatoes on four skewers; set aside.

About 30 minutes before serving, drain marinade from meat; reserve marinade. Thread meat onto remaining four skewers. Suspend skewers across an 8 × 8 × 2-inch baking pan. Broil 6 inches from heat source, turning and brushing with marinade several times while broiling, for 15 to 17 minutes or until cooked through. Cover and keep warm.

continued on next page . . .

Pork Saté continued . . .

1 teaspoon corn- . . . . . **starch**	Pour marinade and broiler drippings into a small saucepan. Stir in cornstarch until smooth. Stirring over medium-high heat, bring to a boil and boil for 1 to 2 minutes or until thickened.
	Serve one skewer of meat and one skewer of pineapple and tomato for each serving. Serve sauce separately.

Makes 4 servings

CHUTNEY PORK CHOPS

1 medium onion, ... **chopped** **½ cup mango chutney** **½ cup apple juice or cider** **¼ teaspoon salt** **¼ teaspoon pepper** **4 pork loin chops (about 1-inch thick)**	In a shallow glass dish, mix onion, chutney, apple juice or cider, salt and pepper. Arrange chops in dish, covering well with marinade. Cover and refrigerate overnight.
1½ cups water	About 1¼ hours before serving, place chops in a medium skillet. Stir water into marinade and pour over chops. Over medium-high heat, bring to a boil. Cover and reduce heat to low. Simmer for 15 minutes. Uncover and simmer 30 to 45 minutes longer or until chops are tender and sauce is thick and golden.
Parsley sprigs . . . . . . **(optional)**	Place chops on a serving platter; cover with sauce. Garnish with parsley if desired.

Makes 4 servings

BAKING RICE

An accompaniment of baked rice can share the oven with any entrée that bakes at 350°. In a greased 1½-quart casserole, mix 2 cups *water*, 1 cup *uncooked regular rice*, 1 tablespoon *butter or margarine* and 2 teaspoons *chicken bouillon granules*. Cover and bake for 45 minutes. Stir in 2 teaspoons *parsley flakes* just before serving. Makes 3 cups.

STUFFED LUNCHEON LETTUCE

1 medium head....... iceberg lettuce (about 1¼ lb.)

From stem end, hollow out center of lettuce, leaving a ¾- to 1-inch thick shell. Place lettuce, hollow-end up, in a medium bowl (just large enough to hold lettuce snuggly).

3 cups diced ham.....
1 small cucumber, peeled, quartered lengthwise and sliced (¾ cup)
2 tablespoons thinly sliced green onion

In a medium bowl, mix ham, cucumber and green onion.

4 ounces cream .....
cheese, softened
⅓ cup mayonnaise
3 tablespoons sweet pickle relish, drained
1½ teaspoons lemon juice
¾ teaspoon dry mustard
¼ teaspoon pepper

In a small bowl, mix cream cheese, mayonnaise, pickle relish, lemon juice, mustard and pepper; blend well. Pour dressing over ham mixture; stir until evenly coated. Spoon mixture into lettuce shell, packing well. Cover and refrigerate for 8 to 24 hours.

Peel from 1 ....
medium tomato coiled in a rose shape
Minced parsley

To serve, place stuffed lettuce upside down in a strainer to drain for 10 to 15 minutes. Cut into six even wedges. Arrange wedges on a serving plate with filling up. Place tomato rose in center and garnish with parsley.

Makes 6 servings

SALMON CREPES

½ pound mush-....... In a large skillet over
   rooms, sliced   medium heat, sauté
¾ cup sliced green   mushrooms and green
   onions   onions in butter or
2 tablespoons butter or margarine for 2 to 3
   margarine   minutes or until limp.

⅓ cup all-purpose ..... Stir in flour. Cook and stir
   flour   for 1 to 2 minutes. Add
2 cups half-and-half   half-and-half, dill, salt and
½ teaspoon dried dill a dash of red pepper.
   weed, crushed   Stirring occasionally,
½ teaspoon salt   bring to a boil and boil
   Ground red pepper   until thickened; set aside.

1 can (15½ oz.) ...... Drain, clean and flake
   red salmon   salmon. Rinse and drain
1 can (4¼ oz.) medium shrimp. Stir into sauce
   shrimp   with vermouth. Cover and
2 tablespoons dry   refrigerate up to 24 hours.
   vermouth

16 crepes (see .... About 1 hour before serving, preheat oven to
   below)   350°. Grease two 15½ × 10½ × 1-inch jelly roll pans
                       or baking sheets. Spoon ¼ cup of the salmon filling
                       down the center of each crepe. Place eight crepes,
                       seam-side up, in each pan. Cover and bake for 12
                       to 15 minutes or until heated through.

Sliced green .... Transfer crepes to serving platters or individual plates.
   onions   Garnish with green onions.

Makes 8 servings

CREPES

2 cups milk .... In a small mixer bowl at low speed, beat milk, flour,
1 cup all-purpose flour eggs and salt until smooth. Cover and let stand at
3 eggs   room temperature for 30 minutes.
½ teaspoon salt

¼ cup butter, ... Blend in melted butter. Heat a 7-inch skillet or crepe
   melted   pan over medium-high heat; coat with butter. Im-
   Additional butter mediately pour 2 tablespoons of the batter into skillet
                      and quickly tilt skillet to spread evenly. Cook for about
1 minute, turn and cook about 30 seconds. Place on a plate; cover. Continue
with the remaining batter, brushing pan with butter before frying each crepe.

Makes about 16

17

LAYERED FLOUNDER HOLLANDAISE

2 medium toma-...... Grease a 2-quart oblong baking dish. Place a single
toes, peeled and layer of tomato slices in bottom of dish. Arrange
sliced spinach over tomato slices. Pat fillets dry and place
1 package (10 oz.) on spinach.
frozen chopped
spinach, thawed
and squeezed dry
1 pound flounder
fillets, fresh or
frozen and thawed

2 eggs .... In a small saucepan, beat eggs lightly. Add mayon-
1 cup mayonnaise naise, lemon juice and mustard; whisk until well blend-
1 tablespoon lemon ed. Cook and stir over low heat about 5 minutes or
juice until thickened (do not boil). Remove from heat.
½ teaspoon Dijon
mustard

2 tablespoons........ Add butter and whisk until butter melts and mixture
butter, softened is well blended. Spoon sauce over fillets to completely cover. Cover and refrigerate up to 24 hours.

2 cups fine soft ...... ⛱ About 40 minutes before serving, preheat oven to
bread crumbs 325°. In a small bowl, toss bread crumbs and butter
3 tablespoons butter or margarine until crumbs are well coated. Sprinkle
or margarine, crumbs over sauce. Bake uncovered for 20 to 30
melted minutes or until fillets are opaque and crumbs are
golden. Serve immediately.

Makes 6 servings

FREEZING PREPARED FOODS

   Food stored in the freezer should be packaged in materials which are both
moisture and vapor proof. When wrapping irregular foods with freezer paper
or heavy-duty aluminum foil, press out the air and wrap tightly, sealing the
seams with freezer tape. Choose plastic containers or glass freezer jars of
different sizes that stack easily and have airtight lids. These are ideal for
soups, stews and other saucy foods. Always leave sufficient room at the
top to allow for expansion during freezing.
   A method of storing casseroles without tying up the dishes is to freeze
the casserole until solid, then immerse the dish in warm water until the con-
tents are loosened from bottom and sides; slide onto a large piece of foil
or freezer wrap. Wrap, seal, label and freeze. To thaw or reheat, unwrap
the food and place it in the original dish.

HURRY-UP DINNERS

> For those nights that call for on-the-spot cooking, you need some speedy combinations. In these menus I have used quick cooking techniques along with some convenience foods to produce delicious family meals. (They are good enough for company, too, but only make four to six servings.) The handy work plan tells you how to prepare the meals most efficiently, all in less than 45 minutes!

Pictured on the preceding page from the menu Elegant Patio Supper are: Crab and Pasta Primavera, Tomatoes Vinaigrette and Peach Sundaes with Almond Liqueur. (See pages 24 and 25.)

The recipes in heavy type in the menus appear in this book.

Preparation Time: 45 minutes   *Serves 4*

SOUTHERN COUNTRY DINNER

Charleston Chicken
Buttered Zucchini Sticks
Romaine and Leaf Lettuce with Oil and Vinegar Dressing
Crusty French Bread   Butter
Banana Cream Parfaits

WORK PLAN

1. *Prepare Banana Cream Parfaits and refrigerate.*
2. *Prepare salad greens and refrigerate.*
3. *Prepare Charleston Chicken.*
4. *While chicken cooks, simmer zucchini until crisp-tender; drain, cover and keep warm.*
5. *Toss zucchini with butter.*

CHARLESTON CHICKEN

"Here's a rich and satisfying chicken dish that has a real gourmet character in spite of its short preparation time."

2 **chicken** . . . . Coat chicken lightly with flour. In a 10-inch skillet over
breasts, boned,   medium heat, brown chicken in butter or margarine
skinned and halved for 2 to 3 minutes on each side or until golden brown.
All-purpose flour   Remove chicken from skillet; set aside.
2 **tablespoons butter or**
margarine   *continued on next page . . .*

Charleston Chicken continued . . .

1 cup sliced . . . .
  mushrooms
4 ounces Canadian
  bacon, cut in small
  strips (about ½
  cup)
1 cup whipping cream
	In the skillet, sauté mushrooms and bacon for 1 minute or until mushrooms begin to soften. Return chicken to skillet. Add cream; cover and simmer for 5 minutes or until chicken is no longer pink in the center.

Transfer chicken to a warm serving plate; cover and keep warm. Boil cream sauce rapidly for 1 to 2 minutes or until slightly thickened (sauce will thicken as it stands).

Watercress. . . . . sprigs	Spoon cream sauce, mushrooms and bacon over chicken. Garnish with watercress.

Makes 4 servings

BANANA CREAM PARFAITS

"If you prefer, try this with canned peach slices, drained, instead of bananas."

1 cup frozen . . . .
  whipped topping,
  thawed
1 cup dairy sour cream
2 tablespoons sugar
	In a small bowl, mix whipped topping, sour cream and sugar until well blended.

2 large bananas . . . . . .
1 cup crumbled
  chocolate chip
  cookies or vanilla
  wafers
4 fresh strawberries or
  maraschino
  cherries
	Into each of four parfait or wine glasses, layer ¼ cup of the sour cream mixture and ¼ cup of the cookie crumbs. Slice half of a banana into each glass; top with ¼ cup of the sour cream mixture and a strawberry or cherry.

Refrigerate until ready to serve.

Makes 4 servings

NOTES:

Preparation Time: 35 minutes   Serves 4

THRIFTY GOURMET DINNER

Savory Sautéed Chicken Livers
Rice Cooked in Bouillon
Tuscan Green Beans
Raspberry Sherbet with Vanilla Wafer Cookies

WORK PLAN

1. *Prepare rice according to package directions, substituting chicken bouillon for the water and salt. (If desired, after cooking, stir in 1 to 2 tablespoons dried parsley flakes.)*
2. *While rice cooks, begin preparation of Savory Sautéed Chicken Livers.*
3. *While livers stand in flour, begin preparation of Tuscan Green Beans.*
4. *Sauté livers; reheat beans with bacon and onion.*

SAVORY SAUTÉED CHICKEN LIVERS

1 pound chicken . . . . . . Cut livers into 1- to 1½-inch pieces, removing any
  livers   green spots and tough white membranes. Drain on
            paper towels.

1 cup all-purpose . . . . . In a small bowl, mix flour, salt, thyme, sage and pep-
  flour   per. Toss livers in flour mixture until evenly coated.
2 teaspoons salt   Let stand in the flour mixture for 10 to 15 minutes,
1 teaspoon dried thyme tossing occasionally.
  leaves, crushed
1 teaspoon ground
  sage
½ teaspoon pepper

2 tablespoons . . . . In a 10-inch skillet over medium-high heat, melt but-
  butter or margarine ter or margarine in oil. When foam subsides from but-
2 tablespoons   ter or margarine, remove livers from the flour mixture,
  vegetable oil   shaking off excess flour. Place half of the livers in the
            skillet so they are not touching. Reduce heat to
            medium and cook for 1 minute. Turn livers over and
            cook 1 minute longer or until very brown. Transfer to
            a bowl; cover and keep warm. Repeat with remain-
            ing livers.

continued on next page . . .

Savory Sautéed Chicken Livers continued . . .

2 teaspoons lemon juice	Drain fat from skillet. Add lemon juice to skillet and stir to loosen any browned bits clinging to the skillet; drizzle over livers.
Hot rice cooked in bouillon (see Step 1 in Work Plan) **Parsley sprigs (optional)** **Lemon slices (optional)**	Serve livers over rice and garnish with parsley and lemon if desired.

Makes 4 servings

TUSCAN GREEN BEANS

"For the best color and flavor, don't overcook the beans."

4 strips bacon, cut in ½-inch pieces **½ cup thinly sliced onion**	In a medium saucepan over medium heat, sauté bacon and onion for 2 to 3 minutes or until onion is golden and limp. Drain bacon and onion on paper towels; discard drippings.
1 package (9 oz.) frozen Italian cut green beans **⅛ teaspoon pepper**	In the same pan, cook beans according to package directions; drain. Return to medium heat, sprinkle beans with pepper. Stir in bacon and onion, heat through.

Makes 4 (⅔-cup) servings

Preparation Time: 35 minutes   *Serves 4*

ELEGANT PATIO SUPPER

Crab and Pasta Primavera
Tomatoes Vinaigrette
Italian Bread   Butter
Peach Sundaes with Almond Liqueur

WORK PLAN

1. *Prepare Tomatoes Vinaigrette; refrigerate. Wash and drain lettuce and refrigerate.*
2. *Drain canned peach slices. Sprinkle with liqueur. Cover and refrigerate.*
3. *Prepare Crab and Pasta Primavera, stopping to turn tomatoes in dressing.*
4. *Assemble salad.*

CRAB AND PASTA PRIMAVERA

"This colorful main dish is perfect for summer entertaining instead of the usual barbecue."

1 package (6 oz.) . . . . . **frozen king crab meat**	Begin thawing crab meat by immersing cellophane package in warm water.
4 ounces vermicelli . . . **or thin spaghetti**	Cook pasta according to package directions just until tender; drain, return to saucepan, cover and keep warm.
1 tablespoon . . . . **butter or margarine** **1 tablespoon vegetable oil** **1 medium zucchini, quartered lengthwise and sliced (about 1 cup)** **1½ cups sliced mushrooms** **½ cup frozen tiny peas (rinse to break up chunks if necessary)**	Meanwhile, in a 10-inch skillet over medium-high heat, melt butter or margarine in oil. Add zucchini; sauté for 1 minute or until zucchini is golden. Add mushrooms and peas; sauté for 30 seconds or until peas are thawed. Transfer about ½ cup of the vegetables to a small bowl; cover and keep warm.

continued on next page . . .

Crab and Pasta Primavera continued . . .

¼ **cup butter** . . . . Reduce heat to medium. Melt butter in skillet with re-
¾ **cup whipping cream** maining vegetables. Stir in cream, cheese, basil and
¼ **cup grated Parmesan** pepper. When hot, transfer to a medium bowl; cover
  cheese and set aside.
½ **teaspoon dried basil**
  leaves, crushed
⅛ **teaspoon pepper**

Separate crab meat into pieces. In the skillet over medium heat, simmer crab meat in a small amount of water just until heated through; drain. Add crab meat and creamed vegetable mixture to pasta; toss gently to mix. Transfer to a large serving plate and top with reserved vegetables.

Grated Parmesan . . . Serve with Parmesan cheese.
cheese

Makes 4 (1-cup) servings

TOMATOES VINAIGRETTE

¼ **cup cider** . . . . In a medium bowl, mix vinegar, oil, green onion,
  vinegar capers, herb seasoning, sugar, salt and pepper until
2 **tablespoons** well blended.
  vegetable oil
1 **tablespoon sliced**
  green onion
1 **tablespoon capers**
  (optional)
½ **teaspoon dried Italian**
  herb seasoning,
  crushed
¼ **teaspoon sugar**
¼ **teaspoon salt**
⅛ **teaspoon pepper**

3 **to 4 small** . . . . Add tomatoes and stir gently until well coated.
  tomatoes, sliced Refrigerate for 10 to 15 minutes. Turn tomatoes in the
  (about 2 cups) marinade; refrigerate 10 to 15 minutes longer.

Bibb or Boston . . . . . Line a serving plate with lettuce and top with tomatoes.
  lettuce leaves Serve remaining dressing separately or refrigerate in
  a tightly covered container for another use.

Makes 4 servings

Preparation Time: 45 minutes   *Serves 6*

ALPINE DINNER

Tangy Alsace Chicken
Buttered Egg Noodles
Leaf Spinach
Mixed Greens with Sour Cream and Onion Dressing
Easy Black Forest Cake

WORK PLAN

1. *Prepare and bake Easy Black Forest Cake; let cool.*
2. *Prepare salad greens and refrigerate.*
3. *Begin cooking frozen leaf spinach according to package directions.*
4. *While spinach cooks, prepare Tangy Alsace Chicken.*
5. *While chicken browns, begin cooking noodles according to package directions.*
6. *Drain spinach and noodles, toss each separately with butter; cover and keep warm.*
7. *Assemble cake and place in freezer until serving time.*

TANGY ALSACE CHICKEN

"Vinegar is the ingredient that gives this saucy chicken its tang."

3 **chicken breasts,** .... **boned, skinned** **and halved** ¼ **teaspoon pepper** **All-purpose flour** 3 **medium cloves** **garlic, unpeeled** 3 **tablespoons butter or** **margarine**	Sprinkle chicken with pepper and coat lightly with flour. In a 10-inch skillet over medium heat, brown chicken with garlic in butter or margarine for 2 to 3 minutes on each side or until golden brown.
¼ **cup water** .... 1 **tablespoon red wine** **vinegar**	Add water and vinegar; cover and simmer for 5 minutes or until chicken is no longer pink in the center. Remove chicken from liquid; set aside. Crush garlic, discard skin and mash softened garlic into liquid.

continued on next page . . .

Tangy Alsace Chicken continued . . .

1 cup water	In a small bowl, stir water, tomato paste, cornstarch,
2 tablespoons tomato paste	vinegar and bouillon until smooth. Pour into skillet and
1 tablespoon cornstarch	bring to a boil, stirring constantly. Boil for 1 minute or
1 tablespoon red wine vinegar	until slightly thickened.
2 teaspoons chicken bouillon granules	

Return chicken breasts and any accumulated liquid to skillet and heat through in sauce.

Hot buttered . . . . noodles	Serve chicken and sauce over a bed of noodles.

Makes 6 servings

EASY BLACK FOREST CAKE

3 large eggs	Preheat oven to 450°. Grease a 9 × 5 × 3-inch loaf
½ cup sugar	pan. Line the pan with waxed paper, smoothing the
¼ cup all-purpose flour	excess at the corners. Grease the waxed paper; set
¼ cup unsweetened cocoa powder	pan aside. In a small mixer bowl at low speed, beat
1 teaspoon baking powder	eggs, sugar, flour, cocoa powder, baking powder and
¼ teaspoon vanilla extract	vanilla until flour is moistened. Scrape sides of bowl and beat at high speed for 2 minutes or until no lumps remain and batter is light and foamy.

Pour batter into pan and bake in lower third of oven for 10 to 12 minutes or until top is evenly rounded and a wooden pick inserted in center comes out clean. Remove from oven and let stand for 1 to 2 minutes (cake will fall and be level on top). Remove from pan, peel off waxed paper and cool on a wire rack.

1 can (21 oz.) . . . . cherry pie filling	Slice cake horizontally to make two thin layers. Place bottom layer on a serving plate and spoon half of the
1 cup frozen whipped topping, thawed	pie filling over cake. Place second layer over filling and spread with whipped topping, reserving about 3 tablespoons for garnish. Spoon on remaining pie filling. Garnish with reserved whipped topping. Place cake in freezer until ready to serve (no more than 1 hour).

To serve, cut crosswise into 1½-inch slices.

Makes 6 servings

27

Preparation Time: 40 minutes   *Serves 4*

FRIDAY NIGHT DINNER

Sole Roulades with Herb Topping
Broccoli Spears
Fresh Tomato Wedges
Crusty Sesame Bread Sticks
Chocolate Creme Fondue

WORK PLAN

1. *Prepare Chocolate Creme Fondue sauce. Rinse and drain fruit; cover and set aside.*
2. *While fondue heats, prepare Sole Roulades with Herb Topping.*
3. *While fish simmers, cook frozen broccoli according to package directions.*
4. *Cut tomatoes and refrigerate.*
5. *While fish bakes, transfer fondue sauce to a serving dish; cover and set aside.*

SOLE ROULADES WITH HERB TOPPING

"Fresh, firm fish fillets work best in a recipe like this where they have to be rolled. I happen to think dill weed is one of the best seasonings for mild fish, especially in a creamy sauce."

4 sole or other . . . . **white fish fillets** **(about 1½ lb.)** **Salt**	Rinse fish and drain on paper towels. Sprinkle the dark side of each fillet lightly with salt; set aside.
2 tablespoons . . . . **butter or margarine** **1 cup chopped onion**	In a 10-inch skillet over medium heat, melt butter or margarine. Stir in onion until well coated; cover and cook for 3 minutes or until onion begins to soften.
½ cup mayonnaise . . . . **⅓ cup dairy sour cream** **2 tablespoons milk** **½ teaspoon dried dill** **weed** **¼ teaspoon salt** **⅛ teaspoon pepper**	Meanwhile, in a small bowl, mix mayonnaise, sour cream, milk, dill weed, salt and pepper until smooth. Spread about 1 tablespoon of the sauce on the salted side of each fillet. With sauce-side up, roll fillets, starting from the thickest end.

continued on next page . . .

Preheat oven to 400°. Stir onion and arrange fish rolls in skillet, seam-side down, on top of onion. Reduce heat to low, cover tightly and steam fish for 10 to 15 minutes or until fish is opaque.

Transfer fish and onion to an ovenproof serving dish. Spoon remaining sauce over fish. Bake for 5 minutes or until hot and bubbly.

Watercress . . . . **sprigs** **Lemon wedges**	Garnish with watercress and lemon.

Makes 4 servings

CHOCOLATE CREME FONDUE

"You can substitute cubes of pound cake for the fresh fruit."

1 jar (7 oz.) . . . . **marshmallow creme** **1 package (6 oz.) semi-sweet chocolate chips (1 cup)** **½ cup milk**	In a heavy or non-stick medium saucepan over low heat, combine marshmallow creme, chocolate chips and milk. Cook, stirring frequently, for 25 to 30 minutes or until chocolate is completely melted and fondue is dark and smooth. Pour into a serving bowl and let stand covered until ready to serve.
Strawberries . . . . **and grapes**	To serve, spear fruit with a fondue fork and dip into warm fondue. Cover and store leftover fondue in the refrigerator. Reheat and use as a sauce for ice cream or pears, or use straight from the refrigerator in hot or cold milk.

Makes 2 cups

NOTES:

Preparation Time: 35 minutes   Serves 4

INDOOR BARBECUE

Texas-Style Smoky Flank Steak
Hash-Browned Potatoes
Romaine and Cherry Tomatoes with Buttermilk Dressing
Cakes Suzette

WORK PLAN

1. *Prepare Cakes Suzette, keeping sauce separate.*
2. *Begin cooking frozen hash-browned potatoes according to package directions.*
3. *While potatoes cook, prepare Texas-Style Smoky Flank Steak, stirring potatoes as needed.*
4. *While steak broils, prepare salad.*
5. *Slice steak.*

TEXAS-STYLE SMOKY FLANK STEAK

"Even without charcoal, this steak has a hearty outdoor flavor."

1 beef flank steak .... **(1½ lb.)**	Slash fatty ends of steak at 1-inch intervals to prevent curling. Place on broiler pan fitted with rack; set aside.
3 tablespoons .... **butter or margarine** **1 large onion, cut in** **¼-inch thick rings** **(about 4 cups)**	In a medium saucepan over medium-low heat, melt butter or margarine. Add onion and toss until onion is well coated. Cover and cook for 5 minutes or until onion is limp. Remove cover and continue cooking, stirring frequently, 7 minutes longer or until golden brown.
2 to 3 tablespoons .... **hickory smoke** **barbecue sauce**	Meanwhile, preheat broiler. Brush steak on one side with about half of the barbecue sauce and broil 5 to 6 inches from heat source for 6 to 7 minutes. Turn steak; brush with remaining sauce and broil 6 to 7 minutes longer for medium rare or until desired doneness. Remove from broiler and let stand for 2 to 3 minutes before slicing.
1 cup hickory .... **smoke barbecue** **sauce**	Stir barbecue sauce into onion.

continued on next page . . .

Texas-Style Smoky Flank Steak continued . . .

To serve, slice meat across the grain very thinly and on a slight angle. Place strips of the meat on a warm serving platter with any juice that accumulated from slicing and top with onion sauce.

Makes 4 large servings

CAKES SUZETTE

"If you're using frozen pound cake, slice it while it's frozen. The slices will thaw quickly and you can return the unused cake to the freezer."

¼ **cup sugar** . . . . In a small skillet, place sugar, orange juice and but-
¼ **cup orange juice** ter. Cook and stir over medium-low heat until butter
¼ **cup butter, cut in** melts. Simmer, without stirring, for 5 minutes or until
    pieces mixture is golden and syrupy; cover and keep warm.

4 **slices (4 × 2½** . . . . . Place slices of cake on individual dessert plates. Ar-
    × ¾-**inch each)** range six orange segments on each slice; refrigerate
    pound cake until ready to serve.
1 **can (11 oz.) mandarin**
    orange segments,
    drained

    Fresh mint . . . . To serve, spoon 2 tablespoons of the warm sauce over
    leaves (optional) each slice of cake, coating orange segments com-
    pletely. Garnish with mint leaves if desired.

Makes 4 servings

Preparation Time: 30 minutes   *Serves 4*

CHINESE SPECIAL

Stir-Fried Pork and Green Onions
White Rice
Sautéed Sesame Cabbage
Pineapple Chunks in White Creme de Menthe
Fortune Cookies

WORK PLAN

1. *Prepare rice according to package directions but without salt (the stir-fry will provide enough salt).*
2. *While the rice cooks, prepare Sautéed Sesame Cabbage.*
3. *In the same skillet, prepare Stir-Fried Pork and Green Onions.*
4. *While stir-fry simmers, drain pineapple chunks; sprinkle with creme de menthe and refrigerate.*

STIR-FRIED PORK AND GREEN ONIONS

1 **pork tenderloin** . . . . . (¾ to 1 lb.)	Remove white tendon from pork and slice ⅛-inch thick; set aside.
1 **cup water** . . . . 3 **tablespoons soy sauce** 1½ **tablespoons cornstarch** 1 **teaspoon sugar**	In a small bowl, stir water, soy sauce, cornstarch and sugar until sugar dissolves; set aside.

continued on next page . . .

Stir-Fried Pork and Green Onions continued . . .

1 **cup sliced green** . . . . **onions** 1 **large green pepper,** **cut in 1-inch pieces** 1 **teaspoon minced** **garlic** 1 **tablespoon vegetable** **oil**	In a 10-inch skillet over medium-high heat, stir-fry green onions, green pepper and garlic in oil for 30 seconds or just until onions are limp. Transfer to a small bowl; set aside.
1 **tablespoon vege-** . . . **table oil**	In the skillet over medium-high heat, stir-fry pork in oil for 2 to 3 minutes or until pork loses its pink color and no longer sticks to the skillet. Reduce heat to low and add vegetables. Stir sauce mixture and pour over meat and vegetables. Cook, stirring constantly, until liquid comes to a boil. Cover and simmer for 3 to 5 minutes or until green pepper is crisp-tender.
Hot cooked . . . . **white rice**	Serve with rice.

Makes 4 (¾-cup) servings

SAUTÉED SESAME CABBAGE

"Sesame seeds may be toasted in larger quantities and stored in the refrigerator for future use. Sprinkle them in salads for a nutty flavor."

1 **tablespoon** . . . . **sesame seeds**	In a 10-inch skillet over medium heat, toast seeds, stirring frequently, for about 2 minutes or until golden brown. Transfer to a small bowl; set aside.
2 **tablespoons** . . . . **butter or margarine** 1 **head (1 lb.) Chinese** **cabbage, halved** **lengthwise and** **sliced ¼-inch thick** ¼ **teaspoon salt** ⅛ **teaspoon pepper**	Increase heat to high, melt butter or margarine in the skillet. Add cabbage. Sprinkle with salt and pepper and sauté for 2 to 3 minutes or until white parts of leaves are crisp-tender. Transfer cabbage to a serving dish; cover and keep warm.
	To serve, drain off any liquid that has accumulated and sprinkle with toasted sesame seeds.

Makes 4 (½-cup) servings

NOTES:

Preparation Time: 35 minutes   *Serves 4*

ITALIAN-STYLE FAMILY SUPPER

Skillet Mostaccioli
Sliced Cucumbers in Italian Dressing
Italian Bread   Butter
Orange Sherbet with Chocolate Sauce

WORK PLAN

1. *Prepare Skillet Mostaccioli.*
2. *While main dish cooks, toss cucumbers with dressing and refrigerate.*
3. *Melt cheese over mostaccioli.*

SKILLET MOSTACCIOLI

"The amazing thing about this dish is that the pasta cooks right in the sauce and you don't have to dirty another pot."

1 **pound ground** . . . . . . **beef round**	In a 10-inch skillet over medium-high heat, cook and stir beef until meat loses its pink color. Stir in mostac-
2 **cups uncooked mostaccioli or ziti**	cioli or ziti, marinara or spaghetti sauce, water and salt. Sprinkle with pepper. Reduce heat to low, cover and
1 **jar (15½ oz.) marinara or spaghetti sauce**	simmer for 30 minutes or until pasta is tender, stirring every 10 minutes to prevent sticking.
1½ **cups water**	
¼ **teaspoon salt**	
Pepper	
4 **ounces mozza-** . . . . . **rella cheese, shredded (1 cup)**	Transfer ground beef and pasta mixture to a warm serving plate, sprinkle with mozzarella and cover loosely with foil for 1 to 2 minutes or until cheese melts.
Grated Parmesan . . . **cheese**	Serve with Parmesan cheese.

Makes 4 (1½-cup) servings

NOTES:

ORGANIZED ENTERTAINING

In these busy times it is tempting to put off entertaining because of the amount of time and work involved. But once you have come up with a workable menu, a good deal of the pressure is off and you can repeat the same meal with several groups at intervals you can handle. Here are menu ideas for various occasions. They are planned to serve from four to twelve people. The style and timing for each menu is different and a work plan is suggested. Read through the chapter and see what works for you.

Pictured on the preceding page from the menu Special Occasion Dinner are: Rack of Lamb, Spinach-Topped Tomatoes (see below and page 37) and Quicker Croissants. (See page 58.)

The recipes in heavy type in the menus appear in this book.

This dinner is as pretty as a picture and tastes as good as it looks. Arrange the meat and vegetables on one platter for a spectacular presentation. Although this is all made in one day, the hostess has plenty of time in the afternoon to relax before finishing the cooking. Get out your best dinnerware for a festive evening.

Serves 4

SPECIAL OCCASION DINNER

Rack of Lamb
Oven-Roasted Potatoes
Spinach-Topped Tomatoes
Green Salad   Choice of Dressing
Hot Rolls   Butter
Cherry Vanilla Ice Cream with Almond Liqueur

WORK PLAN

Up to 6 hours before serving:
1. *Prepare Rack of Lamb for roasting. Cover and refrigerate.*
2. *Prepare spinach mixture for tomatoes. Cover and refrigerate.*
3. *Wash and crisp salad greens.*
4. *Peel potatoes. Cover with cold water and refrigerate.*
About 1½ hours before serving:
1. *Roast lamb and potatoes.*
About 40 minutes before serving:
1. *Complete and bake tomatoes with lamb and potatoes.*
About 15 minutes before serving:
1. *Arrange salad.*
2. *Heat rolls in oven while lamb stands.*

RACK OF LAMB

1 tablespoon . . . . butter, softened 1 teaspoon dried marjoram leaves, crushed ½ teaspoon salt 1 clove garlic, minced Pepper 2 racks of lamb (allow 2 or 3 ribs per serving depending on size)	In a small bowl, mix butter, marjoram, salt, garlic and pepper to a paste. Rub over meat and place, fat-side up, in a shallow roasting pan. Cover and refrigerate.
Watercress . . . . sprigs	Roast in a preheated 375° oven for 30 to 35 minutes per pound or until a meat thermometer registers 150°. Let stand for 10 minutes before serving. Garnish with watercress.

Makes 4 servings

SPINACH-TOPPED TOMATOES

1 package (10 oz.) . . . . frozen chopped spinach	Cook spinach according to package directions. Drain well. Cool slightly.
1 tablespoon . . . . chopped green onion 1 clove garlic, minced 1 tablespoon butter or margarine ¼ cup grated Parmesan cheese 1 egg ¼ teaspoon salt	In a medium saucepan, sauté green onion and garlic in butter or margarine for 3 minutes or until onion is limp. Remove from heat. Stir in spinach. Add cheese, egg and salt; mix well. Cover and chill if desired.
2 medium . . . . tomatoes, halved	Mound one-fourth of the spinach mixture onto each tomato half. Place in an 8 × 8 × 2-inch baking pan. Cover and bake in a preheated 375° oven for 30 to 35 minutes or until tomatoes are heated through.
Grated Parmesan . . . cheese	To serve, sprinkle with cheese.

Makes 4 servings

After a fun outing with friends or a day of sports, it's nice to relax and chat over a hearty bowl of soup and the homey foods that go so well with it. Get your slow cooker going early in the day and the soup will simmer while you're away. The salad and dessert are make-aheads, too. So with just a little attention to the accompaniments and the completion of the soup, supper is ready in less than 30 minutes.

Serves 10

CASUAL SUPPER

Country-Style Pea Soup
Romaine-Apple Tossed Salad
Sourdough Bread   Butter
Date-Nut Torte

WORK PLAN

Early in the morning or at least 5 hours before serving:
1. *Prepare Country-Style Pea Soup (see page 51).*
2. *Prepare Date-Nut Torte.*
3. *Prepare Romaine-Apple Tossed Salad ingredients. Add dressing and toss. Cover and refrigerate.*
About 30 minutes before serving:
1. *Complete soup preparation.*
2. *Toss salad again.*

ROMAINE-APPLE TOSSED SALAD

"A crisp and tangy salad like this is a nice contrast to a hearty soup. The vinegar in the dressing keeps the apples from turning dark."

6 tablespoons . . . . **vegetable oil**	In a small bowl, mix oil, vinegar, mustard, salt, sugar and pepper.
2 tablespoons red wine vinegar	
1 teaspoon Dijon mustard	
½ teaspoon salt	
¼ teaspoon sugar	
¼ teaspoon pepper	

continued on next page . . .

Romaine-Apple Tossed Salad continued . . .

2 large heads . . . .
romaine lettuce,
torn in pieces
3 large Red Delicious
apples, cored and
cut in bite-size
pieces
2 cups sliced celery

In a salad bowl, mix romaine, apples and celery. Add dressing and toss. Cover and chill for at least 2 hours or up to 8 hours.

To serve, toss lightly.

Makes 10 servings

DATE-NUT TORTE

"Don't expect this to have a cake-like texture. It's heavy and hearty and wickedly rich. A modest square with a spoonful of whipped cream will satisfy even the most dedicated dessert lover."

1 pound chopped . . . . .
dates
1 pound walnuts,
coarsely chopped
1 cup all-purpose flour
1 cup sugar
Pinch of salt

Preheat oven to 325°. Heavily butter a 13 × 9 × 2-inch baking pan. In a large bowl, mix dates, walnuts, flour, sugar and salt.

4 eggs . . . .

In a small mixer bowl at high speed, beat eggs for 5 minutes or until thick and lemon colored. Stir into date mixture. (Batter will be very thick.) Spoon into baking pan and spread evenly. Bake for 30 to 35 minutes or until a wooden pick inserted in center comes out clean. Cool on a wire rack.

Whipped cream . . . . .
or frozen whipped
topping

To serve, cut into squares and top with whipped cream or topping.

Makes 12 servings

This special dinner may require a little fussing in the beginning, but it's a delight to serve. Everyone's favorites, chicken and chocolate, are featured in the menu to produce a delicious south-of-the-border treat. If you choose to serve it buffet-style, you may want to provide seating at another table or two. The chicken is a knife-and-fork entrée.

MEXICAN-STYLE DINNER

Serves 8

Nacho Chicken
Seasoned Rice
Marinated Vegetables
Hard Rolls   Butter
Mocha Cream Cake

WORK PLAN

The day before or at least 6 hours before serving:
1. *Prepare Mocha Cream Cake. Cover and refrigerate.*
2. *Prepare Marinated Vegetables. Cover and refrigerate.*
3. *Prepare Nacho Chicken (see page 9). Cover and refrigerate.*
About 40 minutes before serving:
1. *Drain vegetables. Cover and refrigerate.*
2. *Prepare rice according to package directions.*
3. *Bake chicken.*
4. *Remove cake from refrigerator.*

MARINATED VEGETABLES

"These vegetables would be nice with a cold meat luncheon. The dressing has a subtle touch of Mexican seasonings."

½ **cup vegetable oil** . . . In a small bowl, combine vegetable oil, vinegar, chili
¼ **cup red wine vinegar** powder, sugar, mustard, cumin, salt and pepper; set
1 **teaspoon chili** aside.
  powder
¼ **teaspoon sugar**
¼ **teaspoon dry**
  mustard
¼ **teaspoon ground**
  cumin
¼ **teaspoon salt**
  Dash of pepper   *continued on next page . . .*

Marinated Vegetables continued . . .

1½ pounds broccoli, ... cut in ¾-inch slices and cooked crisp-tender 1 can (13½ oz.) ripe olives, drained and sliced 1 package (9 oz.) frozen artichoke hearts, cooked and drained ¾ cup thinly sliced onion	In a shallow 1½-quart dish, place broccoli, olives, artichokes and onion. Add vinegar mixture and toss gently. Cover and chill for 2 to 3 hours or overnight.
2 cups cherry . . . . 🔔 tomatoes, halved if large	To serve, add tomatoes to vegetable mixture and toss gently. Drain and serve cold.

Makes 8 (¾-cup) servings

MOCHA CREAM CAKE

"Here's an impressive looking dessert that almost melts in your mouth."

1 cup butter, ... softened 2 cups sifted powdered sugar 2 egg yolks	In a large mixer bowl at high speed, beat butter until creamy. At low speed, gradually add powdered sugar, beating until fluffy. Add egg yolks, beat until smooth and light.
½ cup unsweetened . . . cocoa powder ¼ cup hot water 2 teaspoons instant coffee powder 1 teaspoon ground cinnamon	In a small bowl, blend cocoa powder, water, coffee powder and cinnamon; add by teaspoonfuls to butter mixture, beating until well blended. Reserve ½ cup frosting.
1 loaf (16 oz.) . . . . pound cake, thawed if frozen ⅓ cup coffee liqueur	Cut cake into three layers. Place bottom layer on a serving plate; brush with one-third of the liqueur. Spread with ½ cup of the frosting; repeat twice, frost sides of cake with remaining mixture. Pipe with reserved ½ cup frosting. Refrigerate at least 3 hours or overnight.

🔔 Serve at room temperature.

Makes 12 servings

For the late sleeper or slow starter, here's the perfect menu for early entertaining. Put the entire meal together the night before, then pop the egg casserole into the oven just before your guests arrive. Relax and enjoy a beverage while the eggs bake and the coffee perks.

Serves 12

WEEKEND BRUNCH

Overnight Brunch Eggs
Prune-Pecan Coffee Cake
Fruit Soup

WORK PLAN

The day before serving:
1. Prepare Overnight Brunch Eggs (see page 7). Cover and refrigerate.
2. Prepare Fruit Soup. Cover and refrigerate.
3. Prepare Prune-Pecan Coffee Cake. Cool, cover and set aside.
About 1 hour before serving:
1. Bake eggs.
About 20 minutes before serving:
1. Heat coffee cake if desired.

PRUNE-PECAN COFFEE CAKE

"If you make this cake a day ahead and would like to serve it warm, simply reheat in a 350° oven. It will taste freshly baked."

¾ cup sugar . . . . Preheat oven to 350°. Grease a 13 × 9 × 2-inch bak-
½ cup butter or ing pan. In a large mixer bowl at high speed, beat
margarine, sugar and butter or margarine until light and fluffy. At
softened medium speed, beat in sour cream and eggs. In a
1 cup dairy sour cream small bowl, mix flour, baking powder, baking soda and
3 eggs salt. Add to sour cream mixture and at medium speed,
2 cups all-purpose beat until thoroughly blended. Stir in prunes. Spread
flour in baking pan.
1½ teaspoons baking
powder
1 teaspoon baking
soda
½ teaspoon salt
2 cups chopped prunes *continued on next page . . .*

Prune-Pecan Coffee Cake continued . . .

½ cup packed . . . . In a small bowl, mix brown sugar, flour and cinnamon.
brown sugar With a pastry blender or two knives, cut in butter or
1 tablespoon all- margarine until pieces are the size of small peas. Stir
purpose flour in pecans. Sprinkle over prune mixture. Bake for 40
1 teaspoon ground minutes or until a wooden pick inserted in center
cinnamon comes out clean. Cool on a wire rack. Serve warm
3 tablespoons cold but- or at room temperature.
ter or margarine
1 cup chopped pecans

Makes 12 servings

FRUIT SOUP

"This dessert-like soup is a welcome change from the usual brunch fruits. It keeps well and tastes better the day after it's made."

5 cups cold water . . . . In a large saucepan, place water, grape juice,
1 cup unsweetened apricots, prunes, sugar, lemon, tapioca and cin-
grape juice namon. Stir and let stand
¾ cup quartered dried for 5 minutes. Over
apricots medium-high heat, bring
¾ cup quartered pitted mixture to a boil, stirring
prunes occasionally. Reduce
¾ cup sugar heat to low; cover and
5 thin slices (⅛-inch simmer for 15 minutes,
thick) fresh lemon stirring occasionally.
3 tablespoons quick-
cooking tapioca
1 stick (3-inch)
cinnamon

1 tart cooking . . . . Add apple and raisins to
apple, peeled, saucepan; cover and
cored and chopped simmer 10 minutes long-
3 tablespoons raisins er or until apple is tender,
stirring occasionally. Cool
for 30 minutes. Refriger-
ate overnight.

To serve, remove cin-
namon stick and lemon
slices. Serve chilled or at
room temperature.

**Makes 12 (about ½-cup)
servings**

Planning a bridge luncheon is always a challenge. I want to serve something special, but I want plenty of time for visiting. This chilled meal is all prepared the day before. The dessert is a rich, flavorful coffee made at serving time from my own special mix. And . . . there's almost no last-minute clean-up in the kitchen. When I serve this, I can really relax and enjoy every hand.

Serves 8

BRIDGE LUNCHEON

Turkey Tonnato
Molded Gazpacho Salad
Dinner Rolls   Butter
Calypso Coffee
Mints

WORK PLAN

Two or three days before serving:
1. Prepare Calypso Coffee mixture (see page 87).
The day before serving:
1. Roast turkey breast or purchase cooked turkey.
2. Prepare sauce for Turkey Tonnato. Cover and refrigerate.
3. Prepare Molded Gazpacho Salad. Cover and refrigerate.
Up to 3 hours before serving:
1. Assemble Turkey Tonnato. Cover and refrigerate.
2. Set up tray for serving coffee.
About 1 hour before serving:
1. Unmold salad. Cover and refrigerate.
2. Peel and slice avocado. Coat with lemon juice.
About 10 minutes before serving:
1. Garnish salad.

TURKEY TONNATO

2 cups mayonnaise ...   In a food processor bowl fitted with the metal blade,*
1 can (6½ oz.) chunk   place mayonnaise, tuna, parsley, anchovies and
light tuna in water,   garlic; cover. Process until smooth.
drained and flaked
¼ cup chopped
parsley
4 anchovy fillets,
chopped
1 large clove garlic,
minced   *continued on next page . . .*

44

Turkey Tonnato continued . . .

1 to 1½ pounds . . . . . . **turkey breast,** **sliced ¼-inch thick**	Arrange turkey on a serving platter; coat with sauce. Cover and refrigerate up to 3 hours or until thoroughly chilled.
Capers, drained	⚱ To serve, garnish with capers.

*If a blender is used, make a half recipe of sauce at a time.

Makes 8 servings

MOLDED GAZPACHO SALAD

"This refreshing salad has a nice crunch inside."

2 envelopes . . . . **unflavored gelatin** **2 cans (12 oz. each)** **tomato juice** **1 teaspoon chicken** **bouillon granules**	In a medium saucepan, mix gelatin, ½ cup of the tomato juice and bouillon; let stand for 1 minute. Stir over medium heat until gelatin is dissolved. Remove from heat.
2 tablespoons red . . . . **wine vinegar** **1 teaspoon Worcester-** **shire sauce** **½ teaspoon celery** **seeds** **¼ teaspoon garlic salt** **¼ teaspoon salt** **2 to 3 drops of hot** **pepper sauce**	Stir in remaining tomato juice, vinegar, Worcestershire sauce, celery seeds, garlic salt, salt and hot pepper sauce. Chill until mixture mounds when dropped from a spoon.
¾ cup finely . . . . **chopped celery** **½ cup peeled, seeded** **and finely chopped** **cucumber** **¼ cup finely chopped** **green pepper** **¼ cup thinly sliced** **green onions**	Stir in celery, cucumber, green pepper and green onions. Pour into a 4-cup mold. Cover and chill at least 2 to 3 hours or until firm.
Avocado slices . . . . . **Watercress sprigs**	⚱ To serve, unmold onto a serving plate. Garnish with avocado and watercress.

Makes 8 (½-cup) servings

45

If you don't want to spend your holiday in the kitchen, choose this easy menu. The dessert can be made a day or two in advance, and the rest of the meal takes only a little over an hour to prepare. If your guests insist on bringing something, suggest a simple dip or a bottle of Rhine wine.

Serves 6

HOLIDAY DINNER

Roast Pork Tenderloins with Apple Stuffing
Buttered Broccoli Spears
Lettuce Wedges with Thousand Island Dressing
Caraway Dinner Rolls   Butter
Hot Fudge Pie

WORK PLAN

One or two days before serving:
1. *Prepare Hot Fudge Pie. Cover and freeze.*
2. *Prepare Hot Fudge Sauce (see page 48). Cover and refrigerate.*
About 1¼ hours before serving:
1. *Prepare Apple Stuffing.*
2. *Bake Pork Tenderloins with the stuffing.*
3. *Arrange lettuce wedges on plates. Cover and refrigerate.*
About 15 minutes before serving:
1. *Cook broccoli.*
2. *Warm fudge sauce.*
3. *Transfer pie from freezer to refrigerator just before serving meal.*

ROAST PORK TENDERLOINS WITH APPLE STUFFING

½ cup chopped . . . .
celery
1 tablespoon minced
onion
1 clove garlic, minced
⅓ cup butter or
margarine
⅔ cup hot water
2 cups herb-seasoned
stuffing mix
2 cups peeled, cored
and chopped tart
baking apples

Preheat oven to 325°. Grease a 2-quart oblong baking dish. In a large saucepan over medium-high heat, sauté celery, onion and garlic in butter or margarine for 3 minutes or until celery is crisp-tender. Add water; stir in stuffing mix and apples. Spread stuffing in baking dish. Cover with foil.

continued on next page . . .

Roast Pork Tenderloins with Apple Stuffing continued . . .

2 **pork tenderloins** . . . . **(¾ lb. each)** 4 **strips bacon**	In a 1½-quart oblong baking dish, place tenderloins; arrange bacon over top. Bake with stuffing for 45 to 60 minutes or until a meat thermometer registers 170° Uncover stuffing for last 10 minutes of baking.
Parsley sprigs	⚱ To serve, discard bacon from tenderloins. Slice tenderloins and arrange over stuffing. Garnish with parsley.

Makes 6 servings

HOT FUDGE PIE

1 **quart top-quality** . . . . **chocolate ice** **cream, softened** 1 **ready-made** **chocolate cookie** **crumb pie crust** 1 **pint top-quality mint** **chocolate chip ice** **cream**	Spread chocolate ice cream evenly over crust. Place scoops of mint chocolate chip ice cream on top. Cover and freeze at least 3 hours or up to 2 days.
Hot Fudge Sauce . . . **(see page 48)** **Coarsely chopped** **mixed nuts** **Whipped cream** **Maraschino cherries**	⚱ To serve, transfer pie from freezer to refrigerator about 20 minutes before serving. Meanwhile, warm sauce. Drizzle with sauce and top with nuts, whipped cream and cherries. Serve remaining sauce separately.

Makes 6 to 8 servings

HOT FUDGE SAUCE

1 **cup sugar**. . . . . In a medium saucepan, combine sugar, cocoa and
½ **cup unsweetened**   coffee powders; add cream and butter. Cook and stir
   cocoa powder   over medium-high heat until butter melts. Continue
1 **teaspoon instant**   cooking, stirring constantly, for 6 to 8 minutes or until
   coffee powder   mixture is smooth and glossy. Remove from heat, add
½ **cup whipping cream**   vanilla. Cool, cover and refrigerate.
¼ **cup butter**
1 **teaspoon vanilla**
   extract

Serve warm over Hot Fudge Pie or on your favorite ice cream.

Makes about 1½ cups

FOLDING NAPKINS

    Pretty napkins can really put the finishing touch on a table. No matter what style of serving you plan to use, find a clever way to fold your napkins and your guests will be intrigued. When I plan to do a fancy fold, I use my heavier napkins. I have found that soft, flimsy napkins will not hold their shape, but can be arranged in other ways such as tucked in water goblets or in a basket for a buffet. Try the taper for a crowded sit-down dinner and the pocket fold for a buffet.

TAPER
    Fold the napkin into a triangle with two points meeting at the top. Fold up the bottom 1½ inches. Turn the napkin over with the points to your left. Roll up from the bottom. Stand upright and tuck the point into the back of the base. Adjust if necessary to make the taper stand straight.

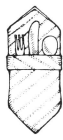

POCKET FOLD
    Fold the napkin to form a square with all the points meeting at the top. Roll the top two layers halfway down. Fold the right and left corners under so you have a pocket on top to hold silverware.

Pictured on the preceding page is Fruited Caribbean Chops. (See page 64.)

SLOW COOKER

HEARTY CASSOULET

"Vary the meat according to your taste, but always include sausage."

1 large onion, ...
  chopped
3 small carrots, thinly
  sliced
3 cloves garlic, minced
3 cans (15 oz. each)
  Great Northern
  white beans

Place onion, carrots and garlic in bottom of a slow cooker. Add undrained beans (do not stir).

1 tablespoon . . . .
  chicken bouillon
  granules
1 tablespoon tomato
  paste
1 medium bay leaf
1 teaspoon dried
  thyme leaves,
  crushed
¼ teaspoon pepper

On top of the beans, place bouillon granules, tomato paste, bay leaf, thyme and pepper.

1½ pounds chicken . . . . .
  thighs or pork loin
  chops, cut in half
1 pound smoked garlic
  sausage links, cut
  in 2-inch pieces
¼ pound bacon, cut in
  1-inch pieces

Add chicken or pork, sausage and bacon. Cover and cook at low heat for 8 to 10 hours or at high heat for 3½ hours or until vegetables and meat are tender.

To serve, ladle into individual soup plates.

Makes 6 servings

COUNTRY-STYLE PEA SOUP

2 packages (16 oz. . . . . . each) dried green split peas (4 cups total)
3 meaty ham hocks, split (about 3 lb.)
4 small carrots, peeled and thinly sliced
2 medium onions, chopped
2 ribs celery, thinly sliced
2 or 3 cloves garlic, minced
2 medium bay leaves
2 teaspoons salt
¼ teaspoon pepper
3 quarts hot water

Place peas in a slow cooker. Add ham hocks, carrots, onions, celery, garlic, bay leaves, salt and pepper. Pour in water. Cover and cook at low heat for 8 to 10 hours or at high heat for 4 hours or until peas are very soft and ham is tender.

Remove ham hocks and bay leaves. Cut meat from bone; dice and return ham to slow cooker.

1 quart warm milk . . . . or half-and-half
Croutons

Stir in milk or half-and-half; cover and heat until steaming. Ladle into soup bowls; garnish with croutons.

Makes about 4½ quarts or 12 (1½-cup) servings

SLOW COOKER TIPS

1. Slow simmering produces a mellow blending of flavors, but remember, whole herbs and spices may give more flavor than usual, while ground herbs and spices may loose flavor.
2. Some vegetables (especially carrots and onions) often take longer to cook than the meat. Place them in the bottom of the cooker with the meat pieces on top.
3. When converting your favorite recipes to the slow cooker, reduce the amount of liquid as the slow cooker lid gives a tight seal and retains the steam. Pour the liquid in last—usually just enough to cover. Fill the cooker at least one-half full for best results.
4. Coating pot roasts and stew meat with flour helps to thicken broth as it cooks. You can also reduce the amount of liquid in the cooker by removing the lid and cooking on "high" for the last 15 to 20 minutes.
5. To prevent overcooking of pasta, rice or tender vegetables such as fresh mushrooms, add these one or two hours before the end of the cooking time.

ORIENTAL FIVE-SPICE POWDER

In a blender container, place 2 tablespoons each *anise seeds* and *fennel seeds,* 4½ teaspoons *ground cinnamon,* 1½ teaspoons *pepper* and ¾ teaspoon *ground cloves;* cover. Blend on high speed for about 1 minute or until all spices are pulverized. Store in a tightly covered jar in a cool dry place.

Use for Oriental Pork Roast (see below) or to season uncooked meat, using no more than ½ teaspoon per pound of meat or poultry. Makes about 7½ tablespoons.

ORIENTAL PORK ROAST

1 pork shoulder blade roast (4 to 4½ lb.)
1½ teaspoons Oriental Five-Spice Powder*
2 tablespoons vegetable oil

Rub roast with Oriental Five-Spice Powder. In a 4-quart Dutch oven or large heavy skillet over medium-high heat, brown meat on all sides in oil. Transfer meat to a slow cooker.

¼ cup sliced green onions
2 tablespoons sesame seeds
2 cloves garlic, minced
¾ cup water
½ cup dry vermouth or white wine
3 tablespoons soy sauce
2 teaspoons chicken bouillon granules

In remaining oil in Dutch oven or skillet, sauté green onions, sesame seeds and garlic for 1 minute; remove from heat. Add water, vermouth or wine, soy sauce and bouillon; stir and scrape bottom of pan until all particles are loosened. Pour mixture over roast in slow cooker. Cover and cook at low heat for 9 to 10 hours or until meat is very tender.

Transfer roast to a platter; cover and keep warm. Skim fat from broth. Pour broth into a medium saucepan.

⅓ cup cold water
3 tablespoons cornstarch

In a small bowl, stir cold water and cornstarch until smooth. Stir into broth. Stirring over medium heat, bring to a boil and boil for 1 to 2 minutes or until thickened.

*Make your own (see above) or purchase in an Oriental market.

continued on next page . . .

Oriental Pork Roast continued . . .

Hot cooked rice.	To serve, carve meat, spoon some sauce over and
or noodles	serve with rice or noodles. Serve remaining sauce separately.

Makes 6 servings

MILWAUKEE SHORT RIBS

"There's plenty of hearty sauce to go with the noodles. Just serve a light, crisp salad with this down-to-earth family dish.

3 medium onions, ...	Place onions in bottom of a slow cooker. Arrange short
each cut in 8	ribs on top and tuck bay leaf into center. Pour 1 cup
wedges	of the beer over meat.
8 beef short ribs (3 to	
3½ lb. total)	
1 large bay leaf	
1 can (12 oz.) beer	
2 tablespoons	In a small bowl, stir remaining beer, brown sugar,
brown sugar	mustard, tomato paste, bouillon, thyme, salt and pep-
2 tablespoons Dijon	per until smooth. Pour mixture over the meat. Cover
mustard	and cook at low heat for 8 to 10 hours or at high heat
2 tablespoons tomato	for 4 to 5 hours or until meat is tender.
paste	
2 teaspoons beef	
bouillon granules	
1 teaspoon dried	
thyme leaves,	
crushed	
1 teaspoon salt	
¼ teaspoon pepper	

Transfer meat and onions to a platter and keep warm. Skim fat from broth. Pour 2 cups broth into a small saucepan.

⅓ cup water.	In a jar, shake water and flour until smooth; stir into
3 tablespoons all-	broth. Stirring over medium-high heat, bring to a boil
purpose flour	and boil until thickened.
Hot buttered	To serve, surround meat and onions with noodles and
noodles with poppy	spoon some sauce over the top. Serve remaining
seeds	sauce separately.

Makes 4 servings

SPAGHETTI MEAT SAUCE

1 cup chopped . . . . In a 10-inch skillet over medium-high heat, sauté onion
  onion and carrot in oil for 3 minutes or until onion is
⅓ cup finely chopped transparent. Transfer to a slow cooker.
  carrot
1 tablespoon vegetable
  oil

1 pound lean . . . . Place beef and sausage in skillet and stir with a spoon
  ground beef to break up pieces. Cook over high heat just until beef
½ pound mild Italian loses its pink color. Drain off fat and place meat in slow
  bulk sausage cooker.

2 cans (16 oz. . . . . To slow cooker, add tomatoes, tomato paste, sugar,
  each) Italian plum basil, salt, bay leaf, garlic powder, pepper and wine
  tomatoes or beer (do not stir). Cover and cook at low heat for
1 can (6 oz.) tomato 8 to 10 hours or at high heat for 4 hours or until
  paste vegetables are tender. If mixture is boiling hard on
1 tablespoon sugar high heat and needs stirring, resume timing when mix-
1½ teaspoons dried basil ture returns to a boil.
  leaves, crushed
1 teaspoon salt
1 medium bay leaf
¼ teaspoon garlic
  powder
⅛ teaspoon pepper
1 cup dry red wine or
  beer

Hot cooked . . . . Serve over spaghetti and sprinkle with cheese.
  spaghetti
Grated Parmesan
  cheese

Makes 12 (½-cup) servings

SLOW COOKER TIMING

Resist the urge to lift the lid and take a peek! As much as 30 minutes of cooking time can be lost. If you must stir, resume timing when the mixture begins to bubble again. Cooking for 1 hour at "high" is the equivalent of 2 to 2½ hours at the "low" setting. If food is not done within the time stated in the recipe, it could be because you live at an altitude above 4000 feet, the voltage is low in your area or you have used frozen foods which take longer to heat. Frozen foods should be at least partially thawed for more even cooking and to prevent possible cracking of your slow cooker's ceramic liner.

FOOD PROCESSOR

CREAMY APPLE CRUMB PIE

"The sour cream filling is almost like baked cheesecake."

½ cup walnut . . . . Preheat oven to 450°. In a food processor bowl fitted
    pieces   with the metal blade, place walnuts; cover. Process
¼ cup all-purpose flour   with six to eight on-off bursts until coarsely chopped.
¼ cup packed brown   Remove metal blade and transfer nuts to a small bowl.
    sugar   Replace metal blade. Place flour, brown sugar, but-
¼ cup cold butter or   ter or margarine and cinnamon in processor bowl;
    margarine, cut in   cover. Process until mixture resembles coarse crumbs.
    ½-inch slices   Stir into nuts; set aside.
½ teaspoon ground
    cinnamon

1 cup dairy sour . . . . . . In processor bowl fitted with the metal blade, place
    cream   sour cream, sugar, flour, egg, vanilla and salt; cover.
¾ cup sugar   Process for 6 seconds or until smooth. Remove metal
2 tablespoons all-   blade and transfer mixture to a large bowl; set aside.
    purpose flour
1 egg
1 teaspoon vanilla
    extract
⅛ teaspoon salt

5 or 6 medium . . . . Insert slicing disc. Slice apples to measure 4 cups. Stir
    cooking apples   apples into sour cream mixture until well coated.
    (Winesap, Golden
    Delicious), peeled,
    quartered and
    cored

1 frozen (9-inch) . . . . . . Place pie shell on a baking sheet. Pour apple-sour
    pie shell   cream mixture into pie shell, mounding apples in
                  center. Carefully place baking sheet and filled pie shell
                  on center rack of oven. Bake for 10 minutes; reduce
                  heat to 350°. Bake for 20 minutes or until lightly
                  browned and apples are almost tender. Carefully
                  remove from oven and sprinkle nut-crumb mixture on
                  top. Return to oven and bake 12 to 15 minutes longer
                  or until brown and slightly crisp. Remove from bak-
                  ing sheet and cool on a wire rack. Best served at room
                  temperature. Refrigerate any leftovers.

Makes 6 servings

FIESTA ORANGE CREAM

1 large orange, ... Finely grate orange rind to make 2 tablespoons;
preferably navel refrigerate orange. In a food processor bowl fitted with
2 envelopes unflavored the metal blade, place orange rind, gelatin and cold
gelatin water; cover. Let stand for 1 minute or until gelatin is
½ cup cold water softened. With motor running, pour boiling water
1 cup boiling water through feed tube and process for 5 seconds or until
gelatin is dissolved. Scrape sides of bowl.

1 can (6 oz.) . . . . Add concentrate, sugar, egg yolks and vanilla; cover.
frozen orange juice Process about 5 seconds or until mixture is well blend-
concentrate, ed. Pour mixture into a large bowl. Chill in freezer
thawed about 30 minutes or until mixture mounds slightly
½ cup sugar when dropped from a spoon.
3 egg yolks
2 teaspoons vanilla
extract

17 to 18 ladyfingers, . . . Cut ¾ inch from one end of each ladyfinger; set ends
split aside. Brush remaining large portions with liqueur.
2 to 3 tablespoons Stand ladyfingers, cut-side down, around inside edge
orange liqueur of a 9 × 3-inch springform pan or in a 2-quart bowl.
Arrange any remaining ladyfingers and ends in bot-
tom of springform pan or bowl, fitting pieces together.

3 egg whites at . . . . . . In a clean food processor bowl fitted with the plastic
room blade, place egg whites; cover. Process for 1½ to 2
temperature minutes or until stiff, but not dry. Gently scrape whites
2 cups whipping into a small bowl with a rubber spatula. Add whipping
cream, chilled cream to food processor bowl; cover. Process for 1½
to 2 minutes or until stiff. Remove gelatin mixture from
freezer and beat with a wire whisk until smooth. Fold
in egg whites and whipped cream until well blended.
Pour into the prepared pan or dish and smooth top.
Cover with plastic wrap or foil and chill at least 4 hours
or overnight.

Mint leaves . . . . Ⱥ Remove membrane from orange with a serrated
knife and slice orange thinly. Drain on paper towels.
Arrange in a decorative design on the top of the
orange cream. Garnish with mint and remove outer
ring of springform pan; cut into wedges or spoon from
bowl.

Makes 12 servings

NOTES:

Pictured is Fiesta Orange Cream. (See page 56.)

SATURDAY NIGHT STIR-FRY

½ **pound beef** . . . . **flank steak, fat** **trimmed**	Cut steak into thirds to make three long, 2-inch wide strips. Place on a baking sheet in the freezer for 30 minutes or until partially frozen.
½ **pound broccoli** . . . . . 2 **medium carrots, cut** **in half crosswise** 1 **small onion, cut in** **half lengthwise**	Cut flowerets off broccoli; set aside. Trim stalks; cut crosswise in equal lengths. In a food processor bowl fitted with the slicing disc, slice broccoli. Repeat with carrots, then onion. Transfer all vegetables to a medium bowl; set aside.
3 **tablespoons soy** . . . . **sauce** 2 **teaspoons cornstarch** 1 **teaspoon sugar** ⅛ **teaspoon garlic** **powder** ½ **cup water** ¼ **cup dry sherry**	In a small bowl, mix soy sauce, cornstarch, sugar and garlic powder until smooth. Stir in water and sherry; set aside.
	Place meat in feed tube and slice. (Do not slice firmly frozen meat.)
4 **tablespoons** . . . . **vegetable oil** 1 **can (8 oz.) sliced** **water chestnuts,** **drained**	In a 10-inch skillet over high heat, sauté vegetable mixture in 2 tablespoons oil for 2 to 3 minutes or until crisp-tender. Transfer to a medium bowl; set aside. Sauté meat in remaining 2 tablespoons oil for 1 minute or until well browned. Return vegetables to skillet; add water chestnuts. Pour soy sauce mixture into skillet and cook, stirring, until sauce is bubbly and slightly thickened.
Hot cooked rice . . . . . **or chow mein** **noodles**	Serve immediately over rice or noodles.

Makes 4 (1-cup) servings

QUICKER CROISSANTS

¼ cup butter or . . . . margarine	In a small saucepan over low heat, melt butter or margarine. Remove from heat; set aside.
4 cups all-purpose . . . . flour 1 cup cold butter or margarine, cut in ¼-inch slices	In a food processor bowl fitted with the metal blade, place flour. Distribute butter or margarine slices over top of flour; cover. Process with ten to twelve on-off bursts until butter or margarine pieces are the size of large peas. Remove metal blade and transfer mixture to a large bowl.
1 cup warm water . . . . (105° to 115°) 1 package active dry yeast 1 cup all-purpose flour ¾ cup half-and-half ⅓ cup sugar 1 egg 1½ teaspoons salt	Replace metal blade. Place warm water and yeast in processor bowl; cover. Process with two on-off bursts. Add flour, half-and-half, sugar, egg, salt and melted butter or margarine; cover. Process for 10 seconds or until smooth. Pour liquid-yeast mixture over flour-butter mixture. With a wooden spoon or spatula, quickly and gently stir just until all the flour is moistened. Tightly cover and refrigerate at least 4 hours or up to 4 days.

On a lightly floured surface, knead five or six times to release air. Form into a ball and cut into four portions. Shape one portion at a time, keeping remaining portions in refrigerator until ready to shape.

Roll each portion into a 14-inch circle. With a sharp knife, cut into eight equal wedges. Loosely roll each wedge from wide end toward point; curl ends to form a crescent shape and place 1½ to 2 inches apart on ungreased baking sheets. Cover and let rise in a warm place, free from drafts, until doubled, about 1½ to 2 hours. (Keep away from a heat source such as stove, heat register or sunny area to keep butter layers from melting.)

1 egg . . . . 1 tablespoon water	Preheat oven to 325°. In a small bowl, lightly beat egg and water. Brush tops of croissants with egg mixture. Bake for 25 to 30 minutes or until golden brown. Im-

mediately remove from baking sheets with a metal spatula and serve warm or cool on wire racks.

continued on next page . . .

Quicker Croissants continued . . .

Baked croissants can be frozen in an airtight container up to 1 month. To reheat, place frozen croissants on baking sheets and bake in a preheated 325° oven for 10 to 12 minutes or until heated through.

Makes 32 croissants

PRESSURE COOKER

SWEDISH-STYLE POT ROAST

1 boneless beef . . . . . . Place meat on a sheet of waxed paper. Rub surfaces **chuck pot roast** with a mixture of allspice, salt and pepper.
(3 lb.)
1 teaspoon ground allspice
1 teaspoon salt
½ teaspoon pepper

2 tablespoons . . . . In a pressure cooker over medium-high heat, brown **vegetable oil** meat well on one side in oil. Turn over. Add onions. **2 medium onions,** In a medium bowl, stir together water, red wine or **sliced** vinegar, brown sugar and garlic until brown sugar is **1 cup water** dissolved. Pour over meat. Tuck bay leaves into liquid. **½ cup red wine or red** Secure lid on pressure cooker according to manufac- **wine vinegar** turer's directions. Cook over high heat until pressure **⅓ cup packed brown** regulator begins to rock gently. Adjust heat to main- **sugar** tain a slow, steady rocking motion (15 pounds of **¼ teaspoon instant** pressure). Cook for 35 minutes.* Remove from heat **minced garlic** and let pressure drop of its own accord, about 5 **2 large bay leaves** minutes.

⅓ cup cold water . . . . . Transfer meat to a platter; cover and keep warm. Skim **3 tablespoons all-** fat from pan juices. Measure 2¼ cups pan juices with **purpose flour** onions and return to cooker. Over medium heat, bring **1 cup dairy sour cream** to a boil. In a small bowl, stir water and flour until **Salt and pepper** smooth. Stir into pan juices. Cook and stir for 2 to 3 **(optional)** minutes or until thickened. Remove cooker from heat, stir in sour cream until uniform. Taste for additional salt and pepper.

Hot boiled or . . . . To serve, carve meat. Serve gravy separately with **mashed potatoes** potatoes.

*At altitudes above 3000 feet, see chart on page 60.

Makes 5 or 6 servings

PRESSURE COOKING AT HIGH ALTITUDES

Have you ever thought of taking a pressure cooker on a vacation trip to higher altitudes? For use on a camp stove or a conventional stove above 3000 feet, increase the cooking time by the following percentage:

3,000 ft.–5%   5,000 ft.–15%   7,000 ft.–25%
4,000 ft.–10%   6,000 ft.–20%   8,000 ft.–30%

For example, at 6000 feet, if the recipe says to cook for 10 minutes, increase time by 2 minutes; thus, a total cooking time of 12 minutes.

MARIA'S BEEF STEW

"Here is a speedy version of a popular Mexican dish."

2 tablespoons all-..... In a medium bowl, stir flour, garlic salt and pepper.
   purpose flour   Place meat in bowl and toss until meat is well coated.
¼ teaspoon garlic salt
⅛ teaspoon pepper
1 pound beef chuck,
   cut in 1-inch pieces

2 tablespoons .... In a pressure cooker over medium-high heat, brown
   vegetable oil   meat in oil. Add potatoes, tomato sauce, onion, water,
2 medium (about 3   salt and cumin; stir to mix. Secure lid on pressure
   inches each) boil- cooker according to manufacturer's directions. Cook
   ing potatoes, cut in over high heat until pressure regulator begins to rock
   half   gently. Adjust heat to maintain a slow, steady rocking
1 can (15 oz.) tomato motion (15 pounds of pressure). Cook for 10 minutes.*
   sauce with bits   Reduce pressure at once by placing pressure cooker
1 medium onion,   under cool running water according to manufacturer's
   coarsely chopped   directions.
½ cup water
1 teaspoon salt
¼ teaspoon ground
   cumin

2 small zucchini, ... Stir in zucchini, corn, parsley and chili powder if
   cut in ½-inch   desired. Cover loosely with lid. Over medium heat,
   slices   cook for 8 to 10 minutes or until zucchini is tender.
1 can (8¾ oz.) whole
   kernel corn
1 tablespoon dried
   parsley flakes
1 teaspoon chili
   powder (optional)   *continued on next page . . .*

Maria's Beef Stew continued . . .

Chopped parsley . . . .
(optional) To serve, cut potatoes into smaller pieces. Ladle into bowls or mugs. Sprinkle with parsley if desired.

*At altitudes above 3000 feet, see chart on page 60.

Makes about 6 (1-cup) servings

PRESSURE COOKER KNOW-HOW

I have found the pressure cooker very valuable for cooking in a hurry and for tenderizing foods. However, it does require certain safety precautions. Practice putting the cooker together, taking it apart and bringing it up to 15 pounds of pressure with 1 cup of water. Call your County Cooperative Extension Agent if you have any questions or don't have an instruction booklet.

My recipes have been written for preparation in a 4- or 6-quart pressure cooker. For successful results, follow these tips:
1. Occasionally rub a drop of vegetable oil on the sealing ring.
2. Look through the vent tube on the lid to check that it is open and clean before securing the lid.
3. Use the amount of liquid called for in the recipe.
4. Fill the cooker no more than two-thirds full to allow for food expansion.
5. Adjust the heat to maintain a slow, steady rocking motion of the pressure regulator.

NOTES:

CHICKEN MILANESE

1 frying chicken, ...
cut up (3 to 3½ lb.)
⅓ cup all-purpose flour
1 tablespoon vegetable oil
1 tablespoon butter or margarine
1 teaspoon salt
¼ teaspoon pepper

Pat chicken dry and coat lightly with flour. In a pressure cooker over medium-high heat, brown half of the chicken pieces in oil and butter or margarine. Sprinkle pieces with half of the salt and pepper. Remove. Repeat process with the remaining chicken pieces. Return all chicken pieces to pressure cooker. Remove pan from heat.

6 medium carrots, ...
cut in 2-inch pieces
1 rib celery, cut in
½-inch pieces
¼ cup sliced green onions

Add carrots, celery and green onions.

¾ cup water . . . .
¼ cup dry white wine
2 tablespoons tomato paste
2 teaspoons chicken bouillon granules

In a small bowl, stir water, wine, tomato paste and bouillon until well blended. Pour over chicken and vegetables. Secure lid on pressure cooker according to manufacturer's directions. Cook over high heat until pressure regulator begins to rock gently. Adjust heat to maintain a slow, steady rocking motion (15 pounds of pressure). Cook for 8 minutes.* Remove from heat and let pressure drop of its own accord for 5 minutes, then place under cool running water according to manufacturer's directions. Transfer chicken and vegetables to a platter; cover and keep warm.

2 tablespoons . . . .
dry white wine
1 tablespoon cornstarch
¼ teaspoon garlic powder
2 tablespoons minced parsley
2 to 3 teaspoons grated lemon rind

Skim fat from liquid in pressure cooker. In a small bowl, stir wine, cornstarch and garlic powder until smooth. Stir into liquid in pressure cooker. Stirring over medium heat, bring to a boil and boil for 1 to 2 minutes or until thick and shiny. Stir in parsley and lemon rind until blended.

To serve, spoon some sauce over chicken and vegetables. Serve remaining sauce separately.

*At altitudes above 3000 feet, see chart on page 60.

Makes 4 to 6 servings

SAUSAGE AND HOT POTATO SALAD

"Open a jar of applesauce and a can of red cabbage to complete this quick German dinner."

3 tablespoons .... vegetable oil	In a small bowl, stir oil, vinegar, mustard, salt, sugar, basil, tarragon and pepper until well blended; set aside.
1 tablespoon white vinegar	
1 teaspoon Dijon mustard	
½ teaspoon salt	
½ teaspoon sugar	
½ teaspoon dried basil leaves, crushed	
¼ teaspoon dried tarragon leaves, crushed	
Dash of pepper	

1 cup water	Pour water into a pressure cooker. Place rack in bottom of cooker. Layer potatoes and onion on rack; sprinkle with salt. Cut sausage into serving pieces, score diagonally and place on potatoes. Secure lid on pressure cooker according to manufacturer's directions. Cook over high heat until pressure regulator begins to rock gently. Adjust heat to maintain a slow, steady rocking motion (15 pounds of pressure). Cook for 5 minutes.* Reduce pressure at once by placing pressure cooker under cool running water according to manufacturer's directions.
4 medium boiling potatoes, peeled, halved and sliced (4 cups)	
1 small onion, sliced	
½ teaspoon salt	
1 pound smoked German or Polish link sausage	

1 tablespoon .... minced parsley	Remove sausage and keep warm. Spoon potato-onion mixture into a large bowl. Pour dressing over mixture and toss gently. Place potato salad on platter and top with sausage. Sprinkle with parsley.

*At altitudes above 3000 feet, see chart on page 60.

Makes 4 servings

PRESSURE COOKER DON'TS

1. Don't attempt to pressure-fry in a standard pressure cooker. Low pressure frying requires some special cooking techniques and safety features.
2. Applesauce, cranberries, pearl barley, split peas, macaroni, spaghetti and noodles are not recommended for preparation in the pressure cooker because they tend to foam and block the vent tube.
3. When cooking rice and dried beans, fill the cooker no more than one-half full.

FRUITED CARIBBEAN CHOPS

6 **pork loin chops** . . . . . Trim and slash fat on chops as desired. On a sheet
2 **tablespoons all-** of waxed paper or in a shallow dish, mix flour,
purpose flour oregano, salt, pepper and garlic powder until uniform.
1½ **teaspoons dried** Rub flour mixture on both sides of chops until well
oregano leaves, coated, using all the mixture.
crushed
1½ **teaspoons salt**
¼ **teaspoon pepper**
¼ **teaspoon garlic**
powder

2 **tablespoons** . . . . In a pressure cooker over medium-high heat, brown
vegetable oil 2 or 3 chops in oil; remove when browned and repeat
with remaining chops. Remove all chops from pan.
Drain off some of the excess fat.

1 **can (15¼ oz.)** . . . . . . Drain pineapple juice into a 1-cup measuring cup; set
pineapple chunks chunks aside. Add water to juice to make 1 cup liquid;
in juice pour into a small bowl. Add brown sugar, onion and
2 **tablespoons brown** tomato paste; stir until well blended. Pour mixture in-
sugar to pressure cooker. Place rack in bottom of cooker.
2 **tablespoons instant** Arrange meat on rack and sprinkle raisins on top.
minced onion
2 **tablespoons tomato**
paste
¼ **cup raisins**

Secure lid on pressure cooker according to manufacturer's directions. Cook over high heat until pressure
regulator begins to rock gently. Adjust heat to maintain a slow, steady rocking motion (15 pounds of
pressure). Cook for 12 minutes.* Remove from heat
and let pressure drop of its own accord for 5 minutes,
then place under cool, running water according to
manufacturer's directions.

Transfer chops to a platter; cover and keep warm.
Skim fat from broth if desired. Add pineapple chunks.
Bring to a boil over medium heat and cook until
pineapple is heated through.

Hot cooked rice . . . . . To serve, arrange chops on a bed of rice. Spoon fruit
over the meat. Serve sauce separately.

*At altitudes above 3000 feet, see chart on page 60.

Makes 6 servings

MICROWAVE MEALS

Microwave cooking is different! It has to be learned. I have spent the last few years experimenting with microwave recipes and this is the first time I have published any. I admit I was reluctant at first, and I will probably never convert most of my favorite old recipes. But being an adventurous cook, the unique features of this amazing appliance continue to intrigue me as I discover tasty new dishes.

The recipes in this chapter are special. They have been tested and retested in several microwave ovens in different locations. They are dishes that turn out equal to or better than their conventionally cooked counterparts. This is a must with me because anything else would be frustrating and disappointing to the new microwave cook.

Before you try any recipe, become thoroughly familiar with your appliance and the basic principles of microwave cooking by reading the manual and cookbook that came with your oven. All of my recipes are designed for 700-watt ovens. Wattage and power settings differ from one brand and model to another. (See the chart on page 71.) You may have to adjust cooking times and settings according to your particular appliance. It is easy to overcook foods when you are not accustomed to the speed of the microwave. Always start with the shortest suggested cooking time and allow for standing time before increasing the cooking time. You will get the feel of it as you try more and more dishes.

Keep an open mind and don't try to force your microwave to do what your conventional oven does better. There are plenty of new things to make in this miraculous timesaver.

Pictured on the preceding page from the menu Double-Duty Family Dinner are: Reuben Meat Loaf and Baked Apples. (See pages 72 and 73.)

The recipes in heavy type in the menus appear in this book.

Preparation Time: 35 minutes   *Serves 8*

VEGETARIAN LUNCHEON

Cheesy Garden Casserole
Tray of Celery and Radishes
Whole Wheat Rolls   Butter
Brownies

WORK PLAN

1. Prepare Cheesy Garden Casserole.
2. While casserole cooks, prepare tray of raw vegetables.
3. Top casserole with cheese and let stand.

CHEESY GARDEN CASSEROLE

"You can also serve this as a side dish with chicken or fish."

1½ **cups instant rice** . . . . 1 **pound yellow squash** **or zucchini** 1 **pound broccoli or** **cauliflower**	In a 2-quart glass casserole, place rice. Cut vegetables into 1- to 2-inch slices or pieces. Place over rice.
1 **jar (15½ oz.)** . . . . **spaghetti sauce** ¼ **cup water**	Pour sauce and water over vegetable mixture. Cover tightly with plastic wrap, piercing to allow steam to escape. Microwave at 100% power (700 watts) for 14 to 16 minutes or until vegetables are fork tender.
1 **cup shredded** . . . . . . **Cheddar cheese** **(4 oz.)** 1 **cup shredded** **Monterey Jack** **cheese (4 oz.)**	Remove plastic wrap from casserole. Sprinkle cheeses over the vegetables. Cover with a foil tent and let stand for 5 minutes. Remove foil and microwave at 100% power for 1 to 2 minutes to reheat and melt cheese before serving.

Makes 8 servings

STIRRING AND ROTATING IN THE MICROWAVE

Almost every microwave oven has a different cooking pattern. You may notice that some of your saucy foods boil more rapidly in certain parts of the dish, or your baked goods rise unevenly. You can compensate for this by rotating the dish a quarter or half turn at intervals during the cooking time. Stirring some dishes or rearranging the food in the dish after it is partially cooked usually produces more uniform results. A wind-up turntable can be purchased to do the rotating for you, but it cannot handle large rectangular dishes.

Preparation Time: 50 minutes   *Serves 4*

SUNDAY DINNER

Chicken and Vegetables Supreme
Sliced Tomatoes
Hot Biscuits   Honey Butter
Vanilla Ice Cream with **Almond Chocolate Sauce**

WORK PLAN

1. Prepare Chicken and Vegetables Supreme.
2. While chicken cooks, prepare biscuits and bake in a conventional oven.
3. Slice tomatoes and refrigerate.
4. While chicken stands covered with foil, prepare Almond Chocolate Sauce.
5. Reheat sauce in microwave just before serving.

CHICKEN AND VEGETABLES SUPREME

"Since the chicken skin doesn't brown, I prefer to remove it before cooking. This reduces fat and calories, too."

1 whole chicken . . . . . . In a 12 × 8 × 2-inch glass baking dish, arrange
breast, split and chicken breast and thighs with the thickest parts to
skinned (about the outside edges of the dish. Fill the center with
¾ lb.) potatoes.
4 chicken thighs,
skinned (about
¾ lb.)
¾ pound (2½-inch) red
potatoes, each cut
in 8 wedges

2 cups water . . . . In a medium bowl, stir water, flour, bouillon, onion,
⅓ cup all-purpose flour paprika, poultry seasoning and browning and season-
4 teaspoons chicken ing sauce until well blended; pour over chicken. Cover
bouillon granules tightly with plastic wrap, piercing to allow steam to
1 tablespoon instant escape. Microwave at 100% power (700 watts) for 25
minced onion minutes or until chicken loses almost all its pink color,
1 teaspoon paprika rotating dish after 15 minutes.
1 teaspoon ground
poultry seasoning
½ teaspoon browning
and seasoning
sauce *continued on next page . . .*

Chicken and Vegetables Supreme continued . . .

1 package (10 oz.)	Stir in peas and carrots; rearrange chicken. Re-cover.
frozen peas and	Microwave at 100% power for 3 to 5 minutes or until
carrots	the peas and carrots are warm.

Remove from oven, cover with foil and let stand for 5 minutes before serving.

Makes 4 servings

ALMOND CHOCOLATE SAUCE

"This will become very thick when chilled, so be sure to warm it up if you're using it straight from the refrigerator."

1 package (6 oz.)	In a 2-cup glass measuring cup, place chocolate,
semi-sweet	water and butter or margarine. Microwave at 100%
chocolate chips	power (700 watts) for 1 to 3 minutes or until chocolate
¼ cup water*	is melted, stirring after each minute.
1 tablespoon butter or	
margarine	
¼ cup sugar	Stir in sugar and salt. Microwave at 100% power for
Dash of salt	1 minute.
¼ cup light corn	Stir in corn syrup and almond extract. Serve warm
syrup	over ice cream. Cover and refrigerate leftover sauce.
1½ teaspoons almond	
extract	

*If desired, substitute ¼ cup almond liqueur for the water and omit the almond extract.

Makes 1⅓ cups

COVERING FOOD IN THE MICROWAVE

Food is covered in the microwave for different reasons. Plastic wrap and glass lids on casseroles keep the heat and moisture in the dish during the cooking process. Pierce plastic wrap to keep it from ballooning. When removing tight covers, watch out for the steam! Lift the cover on the side of the dish away from you. Paper towels and waxed paper keep the splatters down when the food doesn't need to be tightly covered. A paper towel placed under a casserole will catch spills as they occur and make clean-up easier. Aluminum foil is often suggested as a cover during standing time to keep the heat in and allow the cooking to be completed outside the oven.

Preparation Time: 45 minutes   Serves 4

STICK-TO-THE-RIBS LUNCH

Baked Bean Casserole
Cheddar Chili Corn Bread
Carrot and Celery Sticks
Fresh Apples

WORK PLAN

1. *Prepare Baked Bean Casserole.*
2. *While beans cook, prepare carrot and celery sticks.*
3. *Prepare Cheddar Chili Corn Bread.*

BAKED BEAN CASSEROLE

"If you don't have a bacon rack, use several layers of paper towels under the bacon and one on top. You won't have a splatter."

½ **pound lean** . . . . In a 1½-quart glass casserole, crumble ground beef.
   ground beef   Microwave at 100% power (700 watts) for 3 to 4 minutes or until beef is browned, stirring halfway through cooking time; drain off fat.

½ **pound bacon** . . . . Place bacon on a bacon rack and cover with paper towels. Microwave at 100% power for 6 to 8 minutes or until bacon is brown and crisp; crumble.

1 **can (16 oz.)** . . . . To the ground beef, add bacon, beans, catsup, brown
   baked beans   sugar, onion, molasses, garlic, mustard and salt. Mix
1 **can (15 oz.) Great**   lightly. Cover tightly with plastic wrap, piercing to allow
   Northern beans   steam to escape. Microwave at 100% power for 8 to
⅓ **cup catsup**   10 minutes or until mixture is bubbly, stirring after 4
¼ **cup packed brown**   minutes.
   sugar
2 **tablespoons instant**
   minced onion
1 **tablespoon molasses**
1 **clove garlic, minced**
1 **teaspoon dry**
   mustard
1 **teaspoon salt**

Makes 4 servings

CHEDDAR CHILI CORN BREAD

"A moist and tasty way to use a mix."

1 **package** . . . .
   (8½ oz.) corn muf-
   fin mix
⅓ **cup water**
1 **egg**
1 **can (4 oz.) chopped**
   green chilies,
   undrained
	In an 8 × 8 × 2-inch glass baking dish, mix muffin mix, water, egg and green chillies just until blended. Microwave at 100% power (700 watts) for 6 to 8 minutes or until a wooden pick inserted in center comes out clean. The top of the corn bread will have a slightly moist appearance.

1 **cup shredded** . . . . . .
   Cheddar cheese
   (4 oz.)
   Chili powder
   (optional)
	Sprinkle cheese evenly over hot corn bread. Cover with foil and let stand for 1 to 2 minutes or until cheese is melted. Sprinkle with chili powder if desired. Serve immediately.

Makes 9 servings

POWER SETTINGS ON YOUR MICROWAVE

Microwave ovens vary from model to model in cooking power and power settings. The power settings and cooking times in these recipes are based on a maximum power of 700 watts (100% power). If your appliance is less powerful, you will have to increase cooking times accordingly. Check your microwave manual for the wattage at each of your settings. The words used to describe the cooking power (high, medium, low, etc.) are not as important as the corresponding wattages. Here is the guide I use:

POWER	APPROXIMATE WATTAGE
100%	700 watts
70%	490 watts
50%	350 watts
30%	210 watts
10%	70 watts

NOTES:

Preparation Time: 50 minutes   *Serves 4*

DOUBLE-DUTY FAMILY DINNER

Reuben Meat Loaf
Spinach Salad with Creamy Bacon Dressing
Buttered Mashed Potatoes
Pumpernickel Bread   Butter
Baked Apples

WORK PLAN

1. *Prepare Baked Apples, cover with foil and let stand.*
2. *Prepare Reuben Meat Loaf.*
3. *While meat loaf cooks, prepare spinach salad and refrigerate.*
4. *While meat loaf stands, prepare instant mashed potatoes.*

REUBEN MEAT LOAF

1 can (8 oz.) . . . . **sauerkraut**
2½ cups soft bread crumbs
1 pound lean ground beef
1 can (12 oz.) corned beef
1 can (8 oz.) tomato sauce
2 eggs
3 tablespoons chopped parsley
1 clove garlic, minced

Rinse, drain and coarsely chop sauerkraut. Place in a large bowl and add bread crumbs, ground beef, corned beef, ½ can of the tomato sauce, eggs, parsley and garlic; mix until well blended. Press one-half of the mixture into a 1½-quart glass ring mold or use a 10-inch glass deep-dish pie plate that has an inverted glass custard cup in the center.

1 cup shredded . . . . . . **Swiss cheese (4 oz.)**

Evenly sprinkle cheese over meat mixture in mold or pie plate. Press remaining meat mixture on top. Cover tightly with plastic wrap, piercing to allow steam to escape. Microwave at 100% power (700 watts) for 8 to 10 minutes or until meat is firm and has lost its pink color, rotating dish every 3 minutes. Remove from oven, cover with foil and let stand for 5 minutes. Drain off meat juices if necessary. Invert meat loaf onto a serving plate.

continued on next page . . .

Reuben Meat Loaf continued . . .

2 tablespoons . . . . **tomato paste**	In a small bowl, mix remaining ½ can of tomato sauce, tomato paste and horseradish. Spoon over top of ring.
2 teaspoons prepared horseradish	Microwave at 100% power for 1 minute to reheat.

Reheat leftover meatloaf slices the next day and make sandwiches using pumpernickle bread.

Makes 8 servings

BAKED APPLES

"Choose apples that stand straight so you won't lose the luscious filling."

2 tablespoons . . . . **butter or margarine** **½ cup maple syrup**	In a small glass bowl, place butter or margarine. Microwave at 100% power (700 watts) for 30 to 45 seconds or until melted. Add syrup; set aside.
2 tablespoons . . . . **chopped dates** **2 tablespoons coarsely chopped walnuts** **2 tablespoons brown sugar** **¼ teaspoon ground cinnamon**	In a small bowl, mix dates, walnuts, brown sugar and cinnamon; set aside.
4 medium cooking . . . . **apples (Rome Beauty or Winesap)**	Core apples without going all the way through the blossom end. Peel skin one-third of the way down around apples. Fill center of each apple with one-fourth of the date-nut mixture. Spoon about ½ table-spoon of the syrup mixture into center of each apple. In a 9-inch round glass baking dish, arrange apples in a circle. Spoon remaining syrup over and around apples. Cover with waxed paper. Microwave at 100% power for 6 to 7 minutes or until apples are almost tender, rotating dish after 3 minutes.
	Remove from oven. Cover with foil and let stand for 5 minutes; uncover.
Whipped cream . . . . . **(optional)**	Baste and serve warm in individual dishes. If desired, top with whipped cream.

Makes 4 servings

Preparation Time: 40 minutes   *Serves 4*

NICE 'N' LIGHT DINNER

Creole Fish
White Rice
Sunflower Broccoli
Whole Wheat Crackers
Grapes and Cheese

WORK PLAN

1. *Prepare white rice according to package directions.*
2. *While rice cooks, prepare and microwave broccoli for Sunflower Broccoli.*
3. *Prepare Creole Fish; cover with foil and set aside.*
4. *Prepare lemon-butter mixture for broccoli, pour over broccoli and reheat just before serving.*

CREOLE FISH

1 package (16 oz.) . . . . **frozen fish fillets (sole or haddock)**	Microwave frozen package of fish at 30% power (210 watts) for 5 minutes to defrost the block just enough to cut into fourths. In a 9-inch glass pie plate, arrange the fish spoke-fashion.
1 can (8 oz.) . . . . **tomato sauce** **½ green pepper, chopped** **1 rib celery, sliced** **2 tablespoons tomato paste** **1 tablespoon instant minced onion** **1 teaspoon chicken bouillon granules**	In a medium bowl, stir tomato sauce, green pepper, celery, tomato paste, onion and bouillon until blended. Pour evenly around fish. Cover tightly with plastic wrap, piercing to allow steam to escape. Microwave at 100% power (700 watts) for 8 to 10 minutes or until fish flakes easily with a fork, rotating dish after 4 minutes.
	Remove pie plate from oven, cover with foil and let stand for 5 minutes to blend flavors.
Lemon slices . . . . **Parsley sprigs**	To serve, place fish on a warm platter, spoon sauce over fish. Garnish with lemon and parsley.

Makes 4 servings

SUNFLOWER BROCCOLI

"Broccoli cooked in a microwave retains its beautiful green color. The subtle lemon flavor of the sauce is just right with a fish dinner."

1½ **pounds broccoli**	Trim 1 inch from stems of broccoli. Divide into spears. Rinse in cold water. Arrange spears in a 12 × 8 × 2-inch glass baking dish, with flowerets toward center of dish. Cover tightly with plastic wrap, piercing to allow steam to escape. Microwave at 100% power (700 watts) for 5 to 9 minutes or until stalks are fork tender. Remove from oven and let stand covered for 2 to 3 minutes.
2 **tablespoons** .... **sliced green onion** 2 **tablespoons butter** 2 **teaspoons lemon juice** ⅛ **teaspoon salt** **Dash of pepper**	In a small bowl, combine green onion, butter, lemon juice, salt and pepper; cover tightly with plastic wrap, piercing to allow steam to escape. Microwave at 100% power for 2 to 3 minutes or until onion is tender. Transfer broccoli to a warm serving dish. Spoon butter mixture over broccoli.
3 **tablespoons** .... **roasted, salted sunflower kernels**	Sprinkle broccoli with sunflower kernels.

Makes 4 servings

Preparation Time: 50 minutes   *Serves 4*

AUTUMN SUPPER

Sausage-Stuffed Acorn Squash
Tomatoes Vinaigrette
French Bread   Butter
Caramel Pear Squares

WORK PLAN

1. *Prepare Tomatoes Vinaigrette. (See page 25.) Cover and refrigerate.*
2. *Prepare Caramel Pear Squares; set aside.*
3. *Prepare Sausage-Stuffed Acorn Squash.*

SAUSAGE-STUFFED ACORN SQUASH

2 small acorn .... Place squash about 2 inches apart on a paper towel
squash (about 1 lb. in microwave oven. Microwave at 100% power (700
each), pierced watts) for 10 to 12 minutes or until tender and soft to
several times the touch. Remove from oven and let stand for 5
minutes to complete cooking.

1 pound bulk pork .... In a 2-quart glass casserole, break up sausage.
sausage Microwave covered at 100% power for 5 to 6 minutes
or until sausage loses its pink color, stirring to break
up meat halfway through cooking time; drain off fat.

½ cup chopped .... In a small bowl, combine walnuts, bread crumbs, egg,
walnuts seasoned salt and basil. Mix lightly. Stir in sausage.
¼ cup dry bread
crumbs
1 egg
½ teaspoon seasoned
salt
¼ teaspoon dried basil
leaves, crushed

Cut each squash in half and scoop out seeds. Fill each
half with one-fourth of the stuffing mixture. When ready
to serve, microwave at 100% power for 1½ to 2
minutes to reheat.

Makes 4 servings

Pictured is Sausage-Stuffed Acorn Squash. (See page 76.)

CARAMEL PEAR SQUARES

"Use pears that are ripe, but still firm. Test the stem ends to see if they yield to gentle pressure. Soft pears may be brown and mealy inside."

2 **pie crust sticks** . . . . . **(5½ oz. each)** ½ **cup packed brown** **sugar** 1 **egg**	In a small bowl, mix pie crust sticks, brown sugar and egg until crumbly. In the bottom of an 8 × 8 × 2-inch glass baking dish, spread half of the mixture. Press lightly. Microwave at 100% power (700 watts) for 3 minutes or until crust is puffed, rotating dish after each minute. Cool.
4 **Bartlett pears,** . . . . . . **peeled, cored and** **sliced** 1 **jar (12¼ oz.) caramel** **topping** 1 **tablespoon lemon** **juice**	Arrange pears on partially cooked crust, drizzle with caramel topping and lemon juice. Top with remaining crumb mixture. Microwave uncovered at 100% power for 10 to 12 minutes or until pears are tender, rotating dish after 5 minutes. Cool.
Vanilla ice cream . . . **(optional)**	Cut into squares and serve with ice cream if desired.

Makes 9 servings

COOKING ACORN SQUASH

If you prefer not to handle hot squash after cooking it whole, you can cut it in half before you cook it. Cut through the stem end with a very sturdy knife. If you find it too difficult to break through the shell, microwave the whole squash at 100% power (700 watts) for 1 to 2 minutes until the outside has softened a little. Scoop out the seeds and fibers and cover the cut sides with plastic wrap. Microwave at 100% power until almost fork tender. Let stand for about 5 minutes to finish cooking.

Preparation Time: 50 minutes   *Serves 8*
(plus dessert made in advance)

COMPANY DINNER

Salmon Steaks with Green Beans Almondine
Boiled New Potatoes
Crisp Salad Greens with French Dressing
Parkerhouse Rolls   Butter
Chocolate Cheese Pie

WORK PLAN

1. *About 3½ hours before serving, prepare Chocolate Cheese Pie.*
2. *About 50 minutes before serving, scrub potatoes and start cooking.*
3. *Prepare salad greens and refrigerate.*
4. *Prepare Salmon Steaks with Green Beans Almondine.*

SALMON STEAKS WITH GREEN BEANS ALMONDINE

"Definitely a company dish and a special treat for most people. Fish steaks are one of the best foods to cook in the microwave."

½ **cup slivered** . . . . **almonds** **2 tablespoons butter**	In a 9-inch glass pie plate, place almonds and butter. Microwave at 100% power (700 watts) for 4 to 5 minutes or until almonds are lightly browned, stirring after 2 minutes; set aside.
Seasoned Butter . . . . **(see page 88)**	Prepare Seasoned Butter as directed, omitting cornstarch-water mixture and the steps for shaping and freezing.
8 salmon steaks . . . . . . **(1-inch thick each)**	In a 12 × 8 × 2-inch glass baking dish, arrange salmon with the thickest part of the salmon to the outside edges of the dish. Place one-half of the seasoned butter over the salmon. Cover tightly with plastic wrap, piercing to allow steam to escape. Microwave at 100% power for 4 minutes. Rearrange salmon, moving the center steaks to the ends; re-cover. Microwave at 100% power for 4 to 5 minutes or until fish flakes easily. Cover with foil and let stand for 10 minutes.

continued on next page . . .

Salmon Steaks with Green Beans Almondine continued . . .

2 packages (10 oz. **each) frozen** **French-style cut** **green beans**	In a 2-quart glass casserole, place beans and remaining seasoned butter. Cover with plastic wrap, piercing to allow steam to escape. Microwave at 100% power for 8 to 9 minutes or until beans are hot.
	To serve, place salmon on a warm platter and surround with beans. Pour buttered bean liquid over beans and sprinkle salmon with toasted almonds. Microwave at 100% power for 1 to 2 minutes to reheat.

Makes 8 servings

CHOCOLATE CHEESE PIE

3 tablespoons . . . . **butter or margarine** **2 cups shredded** **coconut**	In a 9-inch glass pie plate, place butter or margarine. Microwave at 100% power (700 watts) for 30 to 45 seconds or until melted. With a fork, toss coconut with butter or margarine until coconut is coated. Press evenly against bottom and sides of pie plate to form a crust. Microwave at 100% power for 3 to 4 minutes, rotating dish after each minute. Let cool.
1 package (6 oz.) . . . . . **semi-sweet** **chocolate chips**	In a small glass bowl, place chocolate chips. Microwave uncovered at 100% power for 2 to 3 minutes, stirring after 1½ minutes.
2 packages (8 oz. . . . . . . **each) cream** **cheese, cut in** **1-inch cubes** **2 eggs** **⅔ cup sugar** **1 teaspoon vanilla** **extract**	In a food processor bowl fitted with the metal blade, place ½ package of cream cheese and 1 egg; cover. Process for 5 seconds or until creamy. With motor running, slowly drop remaining cheese and egg through feed tube and process until smooth. Add chocolate, sugar and vanilla. Cover and process just until well blended, stopping motor and scraping sides of bowl. Spoon into crust and smooth top.
	Microwave at 50% power (350 watts) for 11 to 12 minutes or until center is almost set and knife inserted 1 inch from outer edge comes out clean, rotating dish every 3 minutes. Remove and let stand.
1 cup dairy sour . . . . . . **cream** **3 tablespoons sugar** **½ teaspoon vanilla** **extract**	In a small bowl, stir sour cream, sugar and vanilla until uniform. Spread evenly over hot pie to within ¼ inch of crust. Let stand for 15 minutes, then refrigerate at least 3 hours before serving.

Makes 8 servings

Preparation Time: 30 minutes   *Serves 4*
(plus croissants made in advance)

SATURDAY BRUNCH

Fresh Strawberries or Melon Balls
Baked Ham, Cheese and Eggs
Quicker Croissants   Butter

WORK PLAN

1. *The day before, prepare Quicker Croissants (see page 58) or purchase from bakery.*
2. *Wash and hull strawberries, cover and refrigerate. Or prepare melon balls, cover and refrigerate.*
3. *Prepare Baked Ham, Cheese and Eggs.*

BAKED HAM, CHEESE AND EGGS

"Overcooking toughens eggs, so stop just before they are done."

6 eggs . . . .   In a medium bowl, lightly beat eggs and half-and-half.
¼ cup half-and-half

4 ounces Muenster . . .   Add cheese, ham and parsley to the egg mixture. Mix
cheese, cut in   lightly.
1-inch cubes
(about 1 cup)
4 ounces boiled ham,
cut in ½-inch
cubes (about ¾
cup)
1 tablespoon chopped
parsley

2 teaspoons butter . . . .   In a 9-inch glass pie plate, place butter. Microwave
                                 at 100% power (700 watts) for 30 to 45 seconds or
                                 until butter is melted. Pour in egg mixture. Microwave
                                 at 100% power for 4 to 6 minutes or until eggs are
                                 set but moist, stirring every 2 minutes.

Makes 4 servings

NOTES:

Nothing intrigues me more than clever recipe ideas. I find it impossible to resist trying unique new ways of preparing food. Here's a collection of such ideas. Some will speed up your cooking, others will save you a trip to the grocery store or provide for an emergency situation. The No-Cook Berry Jam is one of my all-time favorites and I'm always surprised to learn that so many folks have never heard of this timesaving way to make the best jam you ever tasted.

Pictured on the preceding page are: Oatmeal Refrigerator Cookies (see page 86). Calypso Coffee (see page 87), Food Processor Whole Wheat Bread (see below). Maple Pecan Rolls (see page 85), No-Cook Berry Jam (see page 84) and Fortnight Muffins (see page 83).

FOOD PROCESSOR WHOLE WHEAT BREAD

1 package active . . . . . Grease an 8½ × 4½ × 2½-inch loaf pan. In a small
dry yeast bowl, dissolve yeast and honey in warm water; let
1 tablespoon honey stand until foamy, 5 to 10 minutes.
¼ cup warm water
(105° to 115°)

1¾ cups all-purpose . . . . In a food processor bowl fitted with the plastic blade
flour (or follow specific instructions for your processor),
1 cup whole wheat place flours, dry milk, butter or margarine, honey and
flour salt; cover. Process for 10 seconds or until blended.
¼ cup nonfat dry milk Add yeast mixture and egg; cover. Process for 10
powder seconds or until well mixed.
2 tablespoons butter or
margarine, softened
1 tablespoon honey
1 teaspoon salt
1 egg

4 tablespoons . . . . With motor running; slowly add about 3 tablespoons
warm water (105° of the water until dough forms a ball that cleans the
to 115°) sides of the processor bowl. Let dough rest for 1 to
2 minutes to absorb the liquid. Turn on processor and
slowly add remaining water until dough is soft and smooth, but not sticky, about
60 to 90 seconds. Remove from processor bowl and shape.* Place in loaf pan.
Cover and let rise in a warm place, free from drafts, until doubled, about 1 hour.

Bake in a preheated 375° oven for 25 to 30 minutes or until loaf is golden brown
and sounds hollow when bottom is tapped. Remove from pan; cool on a wire
rack.

*For a finer-textured loaf, place dough in a lightly greased bowl, turning to coat
surface. Cover and let rise in a warm place, free from drafts, until doubled,
about 1 hour. Shape, let rise again and bake as directed.

Makes 1 loaf

NIGHT OWL SWEET ROLLS

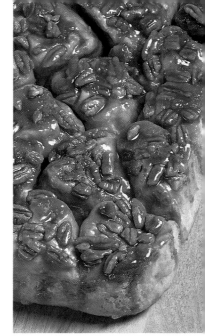

1 cup pecan pieces ... Spread nuts in the bottom
1 package (30 oz.) of a 13 × 9 × 2-inch
    frozen white dinner baking pan. Arrange rolls
    rolls (do not thaw) over nuts. Sprinkle with
⅔ cup packed brown brown sugar, pudding
    sugar mix and butter or marga-
1 package (3⅝ oz.) rine. Cover with plastic
    butterscotch wrap and thaw overnight
    pudding and pie in the refrigerator. Let rise
    filling mix (not at room temperature un-
    instant) till doubled, about 1½
⅓ cup butter or hours.
    margarine, cut in
    small pieces

🔔 Uncover and bake in
a preheated 350° oven
for 35 minutes or until
golden brown. Allow to
cool for 2 to 3 minutes
before removing from
pan. Turn out onto a wire rack over a sheet of waxed
paper.

Makes 24

FORTNIGHT MUFFINS

3 cups all-purpose .... In a medium bowl, stir flour, sugar, baking soda and
    flour salt; set aside.
1 cup sugar
3 teaspoons baking
    soda
½ teaspoon salt

3 cups whole bran .... In a large bowl, stir cereal and water; let stand for 2
    cereal minutes to soften. Add yogurt, oil and eggs; beat well.
1 cup water Stir in dry ingredients just until moistened. Quickly stir
1 container (16 oz.) in raisins. Bake immediately or cover tightly and
    plain yogurt refrigerate up to 2 weeks, baking as needed. (Do not
⅔ cup vegetable oil stir stored batter before baking.)
2 eggs
1 to 1½ cups raisins

🔔 Fill well-greased muffin-pan cups. Bake in a
preheated 400° oven for 15 to 20 minutes or until a
wooden pick comes out clean and top is golden
brown.

Makes 24

NO-COOK BERRY JAM

1 pint fully ripe . . . . strawberries	Rinse and stem strawberries. In a medium bowl, crush berries, one layer at a time. Measure 1 cup berries and juice. Transfer to a large bowl; set aside.
1 package (10 oz.) . . . . frozen sweetened raspberries, thawed	In a strainer, drain raspberries; reserve juice. In the medium bowl, crush raspberries. Measure berries, adding enough juice to equal 1 cup; add to the strawberries.
3 cups sugar . . . . 1 cup light corn syrup	To berry mixture, add sugar and corn syrup, stirring until well blended. Scrape sides of bowl; let stand for 10 minutes.
1 pouch (3 oz.) . . . . liquid fruit pectin 2 tablespoons lemon juice	In a small bowl, stir pectin and lemon juice. Add to fruit mixture and beat vigorously for 3 minutes, scraping bowl occasionally. Pour into sterilized glass or rigid plastic containers, leaving ½-inch headspace. Cover tightly and let stand at room temperature until set (as long as 24 hours).

Jam can be stored in the refrigerator up to one month or in the freezer up to 1 year.

Makes 6 (½-pint) containers

QUICK BUTTERY YEAST DOUGH

1 package active . . . . . dry yeast ½ cup warm water (105° to 115°) 2½ cups all-purpose flour ½ cup butter, softened ¼ cup sugar 2 eggs ½ teaspoon salt	In a large mixer bowl, dissolve yeast in water; let stand for 5 to 10 minutes or until foamy. Add flour, butter, sugar, eggs and salt. Beat on low speed until moistened. On medium speed, beat for 1 minute or until elastic.
½ cup all-purpose . . . . . flour	On a floured surface, knead dough, adding enough of the flour to make a smooth dough. Dough can be kept covered in the refrigerator, punching down as needed, for up to 5 days, or kept wrapped in the freezer for up to 9 months. Thaw at room temperature for 3 to 4 hours before using.

continued on next page . . .

Quick Buttery Yeast Dough continued . . .

Use dough for Runzas (see page 12), Cloverleaf Dinner Rolls (see below) or Maple Pecan Rolls (see below).

Makes 1¾ pounds

MAPLE PECAN ROLLS

½ cup chopped pecans	Sprinkle nuts into the bottom of a greased 8 × 8 × 2-inch baking pan.
¼ cup packed brown sugar ¼ cup maple syrup 2 tablespoons butter or margarine	In a small saucepan, place brown sugar, syrup and butter or margarine. Stirring over medium heat, bring to a boil and boil for 1 minute. Pour syrup evenly over nuts.
½ recipe Quick Buttery Yeast Dough (see page 84) 2 tablespoons butter or margarine, melted ⅓ cup packed brown sugar	On a lightly floured surface, roll dough into a 12 × 9-inch rectangle. Brush with butter or margarine and sprinkle with brown sugar. With the back of a large spoon or with a rolling pin, press sugar lightly into dough. Starting from long side, roll as for a jelly roll. Cut into 1-inch slices. Place slices, cut-side down, on syrup. Cover and let rise in a warm place, free from drafts, until doubled, about 45 to 55 minutes.

Bake in a preheated 400° oven for 20 to 25 minutes or until deep golden brown. Invert rolls onto a serving plate. Serve warm.

Makes 12

CLOVERLEAF DINNER ROLLS

Quick Buttery Yeast Dough (see page 84)	Grease twelve muffin-pan cups. Divide dough into thirty-six portions; form into balls, pulling edges under and sealing. Place three balls, smooth-side up, in each muffin cup. Cover and let rise in a warm place, free from drafts, until doubled, about 50 to 60 minutes.
Butter or margarine, melted (optional)	Bake in a preheated 400° oven for 10 to 12 minutes or until golden brown. Brush with butter or margarine if desired. Serve hot.

Makes 12

FREEZER FRENCH TOAST

6 tablespoons . . . . butter or margarine	Heat oven to 500°. Place 3 tablespoons butter or margarine in each of two 15½ × 10½ × 1-inch jelly roll pans. Heat in oven for 3 minutes or until butter or margarine melts. Spread in pans.
6 eggs . . . . 1 cup milk ½ cup maple syrup ½ teaspoon ground cinnamon (optional)	In a shallow bowl, beat eggs, milk, syrup and cinnamon until blended.
12 slices soft crumb . . . white bread or French bread	Dip bread slices in egg mixture until well soaked and place on jelly roll pans. Bake for 5 to 6

minutes or until underside is golden. Turn and bake 3 to 5 minutes longer or until underside is golden. Cool on wire racks. Place in a single layer on clean jelly roll pans in freezer for 30 minutes or until hard. Wrap, label and freeze up to one month.

Reheat in single layer on jelly roll pans or baking sheets in a preheated 375° oven for 8 to 10 minutes or until heated through. (For small quantities, reheat in your toaster.)

Makes 12 slices

OATMEAL REFRIGERATOR COOKIES

1 cup sugar . . . . 1 cup packed brown sugar 1 cup butter or margarine 2 eggs 1 teaspoon each baking soda, ground cinnamon, and ground nutmeg 1 teaspoon vanilla extract ½ teaspoon salt	In a large mixer bowl at medium speed, beat sugars, butter or margarine, eggs, baking soda, cinnamon, nutmeg, vanilla and salt until light and fluffy.

continued on next page . . .

Oatmeal Refrigerator Cookies continued . . .

1½ cups all-purpose .... flour
3 cups quick-cooking oats
1 cup chopped nuts or raisins (optional)

At low speed, beat in flour until moistened. Stir in oats and nuts or raisins. Mixture will be rather stiff.

Divide dough in half. On sheets of waxed paper, form each into a 10 × 2-inch roll. Wrap and chill at least 4 hours or up to 2 weeks.

To bake, unwrap rolls of dough and slice ¼-inch thick. Place 2 inches apart on ungreased baking sheets. Bake in a preheated 350° oven for 10 to 12 minutes or until golden. Cool cookies on wire racks.

Makes about 6 dozen

CALYPSO COFFEE

"After a big meal, this is all you may need for dessert."

1 cup instant .... coffee granules
1 cup instant chocolate drink mix*
⅓ cup packed brown sugar

In a medium bowl, place coffee granules, chocolate drink mix and brown sugar. With a wire whisk or fork, stir mixture until well blended. Transfer mixture to a 1-quart jar.

½ medium orange .....

With a vegetable peeler, remove rind from orange. Place the rind in coffee mixture. Reserve orange for another use. Cover jar and shake to mix well. Store in a cool dry place for 48 hours or until orange rind is very dry, shaking once or twice a day. Remove rind when dry if desired.

Boiling water ....
Whipped cream, vanilla or chocolate ice cream (optional)

For each 6-ounce serving, place 2 tablespoons of the coffee mixture in a coffee cup. Add boiling water and stir. If desired, top with a spoonful of whipped cream or ice cream.

*Use drink mix which does not contain nonfat dry milk.

Makes about 2 cups mixture (enough for 16 servings)

SEASONED BUTTER

1 tablespoon . . . . cornstarch 1½ teaspoons cold water	In a small bowl, mix cornstarch and water until smooth.
½ cup butter, ... softened 1 teaspoon dried parsley flakes, crushed 1 teaspoon instant minced onion 1 teaspoon seasoned salt 1 teaspoon lemon juice ⅛ teaspoon pepper ⅛ teaspoon sugar	In a small mixer bowl at medium speed, beat butter, cornstarch mixture, parsley, onion, seasoned salt, lemon juice, pepper and sugar until creamy and well blended. Place on waxed paper and shape into a 4-inch roll. Wrap and freeze up to 2 months.

🍶 For 1 package (10 oz.) frozen vegetables, add a 1-inch slice at the beginning and cook according to package directions. Uncover; cook and stir just until sauce thickens.

🍶 Or, use for Salmon Steaks with Green Beans Almondine, omitting the cornstarch-water mixture. (See page 78.)

Makes about ⅔ cup

JIFFY APPLESAUCE

"This is the quickest possible applesauce and has a nice fresh flavor."

2 eating apples . . . . (Red or Golden Delicious) 1 tablespoon lemon juice	Quarter, core and peel apples. Cut into ½-inch chunks. In a small bowl, toss apples with lemon juice; set aside.
3 tablespoons . . . . water 2 tablespoons powdered sugar ¼ teaspoon ground cinnamon	In a blender container, place water, powdered sugar and cinnamon. Add about half of the apples; cover. Blend on low speed until apples are coarsely chopped. Add remaining apples and juice; cover. Blend on low speed, increasing speed to high, until mixture is smooth. Taste for additional sweetness. Cover and chill if desired. Stir before serving.

Makes about 1¼ cups

Index *Recipes photographed

91